1

A. MOHAMED ISMAIL.

AAT Access

Level 1 Student book

Helen Coupland-Smith

Conrad Tetley

aat

Published by Pearson Education Limited, Edinburgh Gate, Harlow, Essex, CM20 2JE.

www.pearsonschoolsandfecolleges.co.uk

© AAT 2010

Edited by Paul Stirner
Designed by Andrew Magee
Typeset and illustrated by TechSet Ltd
Original illustrations © AAT 2010
Cover design by Andrew Magee
Cover photo © AAT 2010

The rights of Helen Coupland-Smith and Conrad Tetley to be identified as authors of this work have been asserted by them in accordance with the Copyright, Designs and Patents Act 1988.

First published 2010

14 13

10 9 8 7 6 5

British Library Cataloguing in Publication Data
A catalogue record for this book is available from the British Library

ISBN 978 0 435049 90 4

Printed in Malaysia (CTP-PPSB)

Websites
Pearson Education Limited and the AAT are not responsible for the content of any external internet sites.

Disclaimer
This material has been published on behalf of the AAT. It supports the AAT qualification, but it is not essential to use this material in order to achieve the AAT qualification. Content from this publication will not be used verbatim in setting the AAT assessment for the qualification.

Contents

Introduction from Jane Scott Paul,
AAT Chief Executive

Dear AAT student member

AAT turned 30 years old in 2010. During that time, we've been one of the fastest growing UK accountancy professional bodies with almost 500,000 people using our qualifications to build the foundations on which to launch a career in finance and accountancy. Currently, AAT has a total membership of over 120,000.

One of the reasons we've been so popular is the support and endorsement we get from employers both in the UK and internationally. AAT isn't about simply getting a certificate at the end of a course. People know that an AAT qualification will equip them with the skills, knowledge and confidence to get the job done. And employers know this too which is why there are AAT members within the finance functions of many household names including Procter & Gamble, Manchester United, HMV and Sky TV as well as local government and the major accountancy practices.

AAT is also respected within education with over 400 training providers in the UK alone offering our qualifications. AAT Access is the latest step on the ladder to help more people enjoy a rewarding career in finance. It has been designed to support the initial stages of your development and provide the essential skills to help you stand out from other candidates when applying for jobs or to support your progression into the AAT Accounting Qualification.

I hope you enjoy studying with AAT and wish you every success in both your studies and future career.

Best wishes

Jane Scott Paul OBE
AAT Chief Executive

AAT – Whatever your goals, you're in the right hands

More than an examining body, we're the worldwide membership organisation for accounting professionals committed to the support, training and development of our members.

Developing skills, not just the knowledge

Through AAT Access, you'll gain a whole new set of skills and understanding of accountancy – needed by every type of business from small local firms to large multinational companies. The skills and knowledge you'll develop can be directly applied to the workplace, increasing both your employability and confidence, and giving you a step ahead in your career.

Accountancy. Business isn't business without it.

You'll learn to calculate and present the business accounts in the appropriate format, as well as how to communicate the story behind the numbers – helping everyone in the business to understand the company's financial position. These are crucial skills for any business professional, not just for accountants.

Opportunities for further study

When you've completed AAT Level 1, you'll have the option to progress to Level 2 of the AAT Accounting Qualification. At this level, you'll start to develop your skills in double entry bookkeeping, sales and purchase ledgers, how to use manual and computerised accounting systems and develop a grasp of management and administrative processes.

Support every step of the way

To give you the very best chance to progress, we're committed to providing training, support and advice throughout your studies and career. Log in to your MyAAT account for study support, access to discussion forums and high street discounts.

Training with AAT means you're also a student member; with professional membership available after you've qualified, our support's there for the long term. And you'll be able to call on our expertise and resources whenever you need them.

"AAT is a good pathway to get to where you want to be in your career."
Lewis Camello, AAT student member

How to use this book

This book is designed to help you develop the knowledge, understanding and skills you need to pass AAT Access. Each unit is broken down into topics based around the qualification's assessment criteria, so you can be certain that all the information is relevant to you.

The following features will help you prepare for your AAT Access exam.

Get ready for the unit by identifying your areas of strength and areas for improvement

Before you start

Read the statements below and decide how much you agree with them.

	Agree	Not sure	Disagree
I am able to add whole numbers and numbers up to two decimal places.			
I am able to subtract whole numbers and numbers up to two decimal places.			
I am able to multiply whole numbers and numbers up to two decimal places.			
I am able to divide whole numbers and numbers up to two decimal places.			
I can calculate the ratio or proportion of two numbers.			
I can calculate the percentage of one number in relation to another number.			
I can find the percentage of a whole number.			
I am able to apply fractions to whole numbers.			
I am able to calculate the average of a range of numbers.			

Key terms highlight important words and phrases and give you clear definitions

Mathematics for accounting features highlight opportunities for you to apply your maths skills from Unit 4

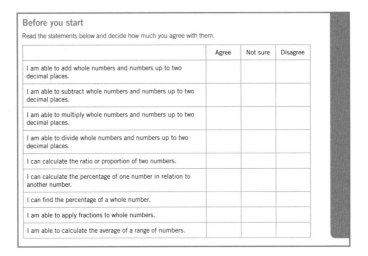

Worked examples walk you through practical techniques, giving simple step by step instructions to help you apply them

Activities help you to develop your knowledge and skills by applying your learning to an accounting environment

Just checking questions help you check your understanding of the topic

Check your understanding ☑

Before you start this test of your knowledge and understanding, review the statements in the "Before you start" feature on page 57 and decide how confident you feel about the topics covered in this unit.

1. Select which **one** of the following statements describes an asset.
   a. An asset is something an organisation receives from customers.
   b. An asset is something an organisation owes.
   c. An asset is something an organisation owns.

2. What is money received from sales called?
   a. An asset
   b. Income
   c. Expenditure

3. Use the appropriate word from the list below to identify each key term being described.
   Words: asset, liability, creditor, debtor, cash sale, credit sale, cash purchase, credit purchase
   a. Someone an organisation owes money to for goods purchased on credit
   b. A transaction to sell goods when payment is delayed
   c. A transaction to purchase goods when payment is immediate
   d. Money owed by an organisation

4. If a supplier allows its customers 30 days to pay, what is this an example of?
   a. a cash transaction
   b. a credit transaction

5. Use a tick ✔ to identify which document would be used in each of the following transactions.

Transaction	Purchase order	Credit note	Invoice	Remittance advice
A customer returns faulty goods				
A customer uses a bank transfer to pay an invoice				
A supplier requests payment				

6. Which book of prime entry would the following documents be entered into?
   a. Credit note sent to a customer
   b. Credit note received from a supplier
   c. Cheque received from a customer

92

Check your understanding

7. Select which one of these documents would be entered in the purchases daybook.
   a. A credit note sent to a customer
   b. A cheque sent to a supplier
   c. A purchase invoice sent to a supplier

8. Show whether the following statement is true or false.
   In an alphanumerical coding system, all codes consist of letters only.
   a. True   b. False

9. Show whether the following statement is true or false.
   In a batch processing system, all cheques received in one day are entered into the cash receipts book at the same time.
   a. True   b. False

10. Complete the paying-in slip.
    a. Two £50 notes
    b. Six £5 notes
    c. Ten £1 coins
    d. Four 50p coins
    e. One cheque for £525.50

Date:	Date:	City Bank plc Redport	£50 notes	
A/C			£20 notes	
			£10 notes	
Cash:		Account	£5 notes	
			£2 coin	
Cheques, POs:	No. of cheques		£1 coin	
		Paid in by	Other coin	
Total:			Total cash	
			Cheques, POs	
000001		30-45-22 10678465	Total £	

11. Show whether the following statement is true or false.
    A paying-in slip should list details of all cheques on the back.
    a. True   b. False

12. Show whether the following statement is true or false.
    A cheque should be signed by the payee.
    a. True   b. False

13. Complete the following sentence by selecting the most appropriate word from the list below:
    same as, higher than, lower than
    When income is _____ expenses an organisation has made a loss.

14. Look at the following table of income and expenditure and answer the questions below.

Income and expenditure	£
Sales	250,000
Cost of sales	130,000
Wages	65,500
Office expenses	25,000
Selling expenses	13,000

   a. Calculate gross profit.
   b. Calculate net profit.
   c. What is net profit as a percentage of sales?

93

Each unit ends with a **Check your understanding** activity, which will help you to assess whether there are any areas of the unit you need to recap before moving on. These are written in the style of the actual AAT exam to help you develop your confidence.

Once you have worked through all the units and completed all the Check your understanding activities, you will be ready to try the mock exam at the end of the book. This is the same format as the actual AAT exam and will help you identify any topics you need to revise.

Good luck with your studies, and we hope you enjoy using this book.

Unit 1: Accounting in a professional environment

Introduction

In this unit you will develop an understanding of how accounting works in a professional environment. As an accounting professional, it is important that you know how your work contributes to the overall success of a business. You need to know how to behave ethically, and how the law affects you and your employer. This unit highlights how you can achieve success and build your career through working efficiently and through personal development.

By the end of this unit you will:

- understand basic organisations and how the finance professional contributes to the organisation

- understand the need to apply appropriate ethical behaviour and professionalism within an accounting environment

- understand that there is a legal framework within which organisations must operate

- understand how efficient working practices and personal development contribute to achievement.

Gethin Phillips, FMAAT

Good accounts departments work as a team to make sure they don't drop the ball.

Before you start

Read the statements below and decide how much you agree with them.

	Agree	Not sure	Disagree
I know what an accounts department does.			
I know the kind of documents that an accounts department deals with.			
I know why I must be accurate when working in an accounts department.			
I know how an accounts department supports the functions of a business.			
I know why I must keep information confidential.			
I know how health and safety laws affect me.			
I know how an employee in an accounting function can make sure they keep information secure.			

Types of business organisation

Key terms

Private sector: The part of the economy consisting of privately owned businesses that are set up to make a profit. These include sole traders, partnerships and limited companies.

Profit: The amount of money a business makes when all expenses have been deducted from turnover.

Shareholders: The owners of limited companies. They invest money in a company in the hope that it will make a profit, so they will get a return on the money they invested.

Public sector: The part of the economy consisting of publicly owned organisations that provide services to citizens. These organisations are paid for through taxation.

Charities: Organisations set up to raise money and awareness to promote a particular cause and to provide services for specific groups.

Business organisations come in many sizes and with different types of ownership. In the **private sector**, businesses exist to make a **profit** for their owners. There are three main types of businesses in the private sector.

- Sole traders are the most basic form of business organisation. A sole trader business is owned by one person, who normally invests their own money in the venture. If the business gets into financial difficulty, the sole trader is responsible for all the debts. However, the sole trader takes all the profits when the business does well.

- Partnerships are business agreements between two or more people. The owners of a partnership, known as partners, take the same financial risks as sole traders but also agree to share all the profits. There can be up to 20 partners in a partnership.

- Companies are owned by their **shareholders**. There are two main types of company: private limited companies (Ltd) and public limited companies (plc). In larger companies, the owners appoint managers to run the business. The owners of limited companies are not responsible for all the business's debts, as they only stand to lose what they have invested in the business.

The **public sector** provides essential services such as rubbish collection, healthcare and policing. These services are financed through the taxes paid by individuals as well as by businesses. Public sector organisations aim to provide value for money.

Charities are another type of business organisation. They are set up to raise awareness of a particular issue. They raise funds to provide services and to research and promote their causes. Any money they make above the amount they spend is called a surplus.

Case study

Mason & Jones Engineering

Mason & Jones Engineering is a medium-sized engineering organisation. John Mason and Paul Jones set up the business as a partnership.

The business has grown steadily, but has now reached a point where it needs to expand further to remain competitive. Without new investment to improve its machinery, the business is going to start losing work to foreign competitors. John and Paul know they can raise money by turning the business into a limited company. However, they are worried that they may lose control of the business they have worked so hard to build up.

1 What is a limited company?

2 Why would becoming a limited company suit Mason & Jones Engineering in its current situation?

Activity: Business organisations

Copy the diagram below. Complete the diagram by identifying and listing at least three organisations in your local area in each sector.

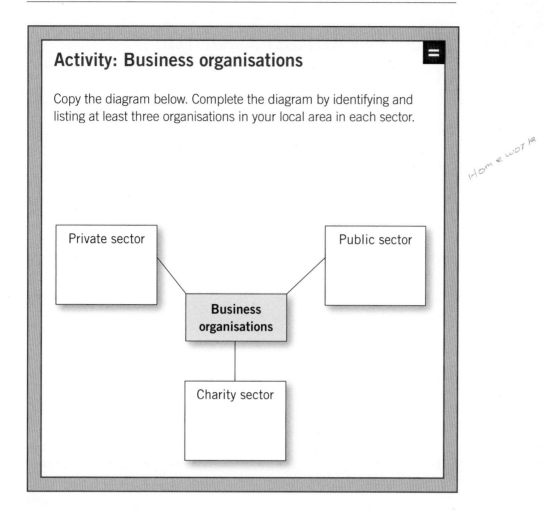

Private sector

Public sector

Business organisations

Charity sector

Just checking

1 What is the difference between a private limited company and a charity?

2 How does a limited company differ from a sole trader or partnership?

3 How is the private sector different from the public sector?

Unit 1
1.2
The "customers" of the accounting function

Key terms

Internal customer: A person from inside the organisation who requests financial information from the organisation's accounts department.

External customer: A person from outside the organisation who requests information from the accounts department.

Function: An activity carried out in an organisation, often in a department of the same name. For example, the sales function is usually carried out by sales teams in the sales department.

There are many "customers" of an accounts department in an organisation. They come from both inside (**internal customers**) and outside (**external customers**) the organisation. It is important that any work an accounts department completes is accurate and meets the needs of all the department's customers.

As an accounting professional it will be your job to prepare the information that your customers require. Here are two examples of typical requests you might receive.

- Someone from the sales department of your organisation wants to know how much profit has been made on one of the organisation's products. This request comes from an internal customer. You would need to gather all the necessary information and submit a report to this person.

- A supplier wants to know when its invoice will be paid. This request comes from an external customer of the accounts department. Again, you would need to find out this information and reply to the supplier.

Remember, anything you provide is only useful if it is the information your customer requested and if it is accurate.

Worked example

Types of customers

Figure 1.1 shows some of the main types of customers of the accounting **function**. It explains their relationship to the business and the sort of information they will require from the accounts department. You should note that the accounting function in a business may also have many other customers. For example, it will have to prepare important information for HM Revenue & Customs (HMRC) and, if it is a limited company, for the company's shareholders.

External customers	Internal customers
Suppliers These provide goods and services to a business. Suppliers will often trade on credit terms. This means they will issue an invoice with the goods and allow the business to pay later. Before offering credit, suppliers may need information to make sure the business is financially safe. They will expect the accounts department to issue purchase orders and pay invoices.	**Employees** The information that employees need will depend on the functional area of the business in which they work. • Managers need to know about the financial state of the business to make decisions. • Human resources personnel need to know how much money is available for hiring staff. • Marketing departments need to know how much they can spend on advertising.
Trade customers Some businesses supply goods and services to some of their customers on credit terms. These trade customers need to know how much they owe the business, and when they need to pay their debts.	

Figure 1.1: Customers of the accounting function

Activity: Identifying customers

You work for the finance department of Kit Fortune, a sports clothes retailer. You have received four requests for information. Read this list of customer requests and, in each case, identify whether the customer is internal or external.

1 Jas is a trade customer and she wants to know how much she currently owes Kit Fortune. She has contacted you to ask for a statement of her account. *EXT*

2 Mark from the sales team has asked how much business Kit Fortune does with Train4It. He wants the information to help him agree discounts and offers with Train4It when it makes a new order. *Int*

3 Aisha from credit control needs to see the balance of Tina Smith's account. Tina is a trade customer who has not settled her account and needs to be chased for payment. *Int*

4 Threadneedle, one of Kit Fortune's major suppliers, has *Ext* contacted you to find out when the invoice for its latest delivery will be paid.

Just checking

1 Who are the internal customers of the accounting function?

2 Who are the external customers?

3 Is HM Revenue & Customs an internal or external customer?

How the accounting function supports an organisation

The accounting function is important for the success of any organisation. If an organisation can't control its finances, it won't survive for very long. The accounting function performs many vital roles. These support many different functions in the organisation.

In a business, the marketing department may want to know whether sales have increased after a promotional campaign. The human resources department may want to know if the business can afford to employ more staff. In one way or another, all functions within the business rely on the work of the **accounting professionals**.

Managers will often check the actual amount of money spent by the organisation against the amount they had planned to spend. Similarly, they will compare the amount of money received by the organisation against their forecasts for income. These comparisons will help them to make decisions about how they should run the organisation in the short term. Because this information is so key to the running of the organisation, it is important that you present it complete (so nothing is missing), and in a timely and accurate fashion. When working in an accounts department, the managers of your organisation will be one of your most important customers.

Worked example

Type of support

It is important to know the type of **support** that the accounting function offers to the rest of an organisation. Figure 1.2 shows how the accounting function helps some of the departments in a business in completing their work.

Department	Support offered by the accounting function
Management	The organisation's management needs financial information, such as costs, sales and profit, in order to make better business decisions.
Sales	The accounts department will be able to advise how many sales have been made and how the function is performing against its targets.
Production	The accounts department will be able to tell the production department how much an item costs to produce. It will provide information to help production make decisions on which suppliers to use. It will help the business set prices for its products.
Human resources	The accounts department will be able to advise human resources on how many staff the business can afford to employ.
Marketing	The accounts department will be able to advise the marketing function how much it can afford to spend on promotional activity. It will also provide records of how much has been spent on promotion.

Figure 1.2: Support offered by the accounting function

Activity: Support offered by the accounting function

Figure 1.2 gives a basic insight into how an accounting function supports the work of other departments within a business. Explore this idea further by focusing on an organisation of your choice. This organisation must have more than the five functional areas highlighted in Figure 1.2. This means it is likely to be a large organisation.

- What functional areas in your chosen organisation – other than those highlighted in Figure 1.2 – will require support from the accounting function?

- See if you can identify the different types of financial information that will be required by each functional area in your chosen organisation. You should cover both the departments highlighted in Figure 1.2 and the other functional areas you have found.

Just checking

1 List three functional areas that an accounting function can support in a business.

2 Which three words describe the way in which the accounting function should provide information?

3 What problems may occur if the accounts department provides incorrect advice to the human resources function on how much money is available to recruit and train new staff?

Maintaining confidentiality of information

Key terms

Confidential: Private or sensitive. The term is often applied to financial and personal information that must be kept secret or only made available to certain people.
Legal: In keeping with the law.

As an accounting professional, you will have access to important information. Often this information will be **confidential**, and it must be kept secure.

There are several reasons for keeping information secure. It is important that some information doesn't fall into the wrong hands. In business, a leak of financial information could be very damaging. If a competitor gets hold of confidential information, it may be able to use this to its advantage when competing with your business.

Personal information about employees or customers must also be protected. If the information contains personal data, such as details of an individual's bank account, it could be used illegally for fraud or identity theft.

All information held by an organisation has to be kept in a way that meets **legal** standards. If an organisation doesn't comply with the law, then it can face criminal penalties. The organisation can be fined and some of its staff could get a criminal record.

Worked example

Keeping information secure

The information that you handle in an accounting role will often be sensitive. This will include both information held in electronic records and contained in paper documents. There are some simple rules that you can follow to keep this information confidential.

Information on paper

- Don't leave documents out on your desk while you are away from the office. Always keep confidential papers locked in a filing cabinet or a drawer.

- If you want to throw the document away (because, for example, it is only a printout of information held electronically), make sure that it is shredded before the paper is sent for recycling.

- Make sure you lock filing cabinets and drawers at the end of the working day.

Information held electronically

- Don't leave confidential information visible on your computer screen when you are away from your desk. Close the file, or lock your computer.

- Use password protection, so that the information can only be accessed by those who have the password.

- Don't write down the password for accessing electronic files. It could be found by someone who is not authorised to access confidential information.

Activity: Keep it confidential

Link the types of document that you will need to keep confidential to the best method of keeping it confidential.

| A printout of a customer's credit account details that you don't need to keep any more | Keep the file in a locked filing cabinet |

A spreadsheet of the organisation's profit and loss accounts, which needs to be accessed by certain people in the finance department

Put the document in a drawer and lock the drawer until you come back

An important file of papers giving details of a customer's spending and credit limits over the past few years

Shred the document

A printed document you are checking for accuracy, but you need to be away from your desk for a few minutes

Password-protect the file and share the password only with those who need to access the file

Just checking

1 What does confidential mean?

2 Why is it important to keep some information confidential?

3 What information should you keep confidential?

4 What problems could occur if confidential data is leaked from an organisation?

Ethical and professional behaviour

Key terms

Professional: A person who is qualified to carry out a task with a high level of expertise and skill.

Behaviour: How a person conducts themself.

Ethical: The correct and acceptable way of doing something.

When working within an accounting function, you will be expected to work to the highest standards at all times. The position you hold may carry a great deal of responsibility. For example, you may be handling sensitive and confidential information. As a result, your employer will expect you to act as a **professional**.

Your **behaviour** will be seen as a reflection of your organisation and your work. Organisations that regularly make mistakes and treat others with a lack of respect will soon lose customers and go out of business.

Ethical and professional behaviour is required of anyone working in an accounting function. Accountancy relies on accuracy and trust. It is therefore vital that you complete the work you undertake in a clear and accurate way. Other people must be able to follow what you are doing to ensure it is done correctly.

Professional behaviour in an accountancy context means that you should have up-to-date technical knowledge. You may need regular training to keep your skills and knowledge relevant. For example, you will need training if your employer introduces a new accounting system.

Case study

Ethical behaviour at work

Temi works in the finance department of a housing association. Part of her role involves accounting for the money coming into the organisation from tenants and chasing for payment when rent is overdue. The housing association has a three-step process for recovering money from tenants who do not pay their rent on time.

i) After a week, the housing association sends a letter to the tenant advising that the rent is overdue and requesting payment.

ii) After a month, the housing association sends another letter advising that if the tenant doesn't pay within the next week, the housing association will get a debt collection agency involved and the tenant may be evicted.

iii) A week later, the debt collection agency is instructed to recover the money owed to the housing association.

Temi notices that one of the housing association's tenants is someone she used to go to school with. Carl, her former schoolmate, is five weeks behind with his rent. The debt collectors have been unable to recover the money, and the housing association is starting proceedings to get Carl evicted.

1 Temi is spending some time with her friends. Some of her friends know Carl. Why would it be unethical for Temi to talk with her friends about Carl's situation?

2 Why would it be unethical for Temi to treat Carl in a different way from any of the housing association's other tenants?

Activity: Ethics and professional behaviour

For this activity, you need to complete a quiz that will test your understanding of ethics and professional behaviour. To access the quiz, visit **www.aat-interactive.org.uk/ethics/**

Before answering the questions on this AAT website, first read the scenarios carefully. Then select the response that you think is correct.

Just checking

1 What does the word ethical mean?

2 Why must accounting professionals act in an ethical way?

3 Why is training important for professional behaviour?

Environmentally and socially responsible policies

In today's world, businesses have to think about more than just making a profit. There is growing awareness of **environmental** issues. Topics such as climate change, pollution and **sustainability** receive a lot of media attention. All organisations, like individuals, have a responsibility for recycling and reducing waste.

You may be wondering how this affects accounting professionals. Today, there is an expectation that everyone does their bit to save the planet and help the community at large. As an accounting professional, you can help by doing simple things such as recycling waste paper and saving electricity by switching off computers, equipment and lights at the end of the day.

Worked example

Sustainability policies

Organisations can change how they work to be more environmentally and socially responsible. Below are some typical sustainability **policies** that many organisations have introduced.

- Recycling policies – an organisation may have a policy to recycle all paper, cardboard, plastics, glass, printer cartridges and other materials it uses.

- Energy-saving policies – an organisation may have a policy to cut down on its energy usage by replacing light bulbs with energy-efficient bulbs and by installing motion sensors that automatically switch off lights if there is nobody in the room.

- Fuel-efficiency policies – an organisation may try to cut down on staff travel for business purposes by installing video or phone conferencing facilities.

Some organisations also encourage their employees to be more environmentally aware. They might provide incentives for staff to cycle to work, or organise car sharing schemes.

Karen Liddle, Procter & Gamble, Accredited employer

Some large organisations publish their environmentally and socially responsible policies.

Activity: Environmentally and socially responsible

Stoat's Accountants is a nationwide accountancy business with five offices across the UK. It has recently adopted an environmental and social responsibility policy.

This includes:
- printing documents double-sided to reduce paper waste
- providing staff with recycling facilities for paper, plastic and aluminium
- installing energy-saving light bulbs
- asking staff to use telephone and video conferencing facilities rather than drive to meetings.

1 Has your training provider taken any of the above steps to improve its environmental and social responsibility?

2 Are there any additional steps your training provider could take?

3 Are there any steps your training provider has taken that Stoat's Accountants could take?

Just checking

1 Explain what being environmentally and socially responsible means.

2 Why would an organisation want to act in an environmentally and socially responsible way?

3 How might a policy of acting in an environmentally and socially responsible manner benefit an accounting organisation?

Health and safety

The **health and safety** of everyone in the workplace is extremely important. An employer may be **liable** for any injuries caused at work. This means that if the employer is found to have been **responsible** for an injury, legal action may be taken against the organisation. However, health and safety is the responsibility of not just the employer but also the employees. Everyone in the workplace is responsible for maintaining health and safety.

If you need to carry out any jobs that carry the risk of injury, you must be trained properly. These jobs include carrying heavy loads, changing potentially dangerous printer ink cartridges, and using unfamiliar chemicals to clean computer equipment.

You are also responsible for those around you at work. If you see something that might cause someone harm, you need to do something about it. For example, if you see wires from a computer trailing into the walkway, you have a responsibility to tidy the wires away. If left trailing, these wires could trip someone up. If you can't take action yourself, you should tell somebody in the workplace who can make the situation safe.

Case study

Jones & Mooring Partnership

Jones & Mooring Partnership is a well-established accountancy business. It employs 20 staff and occupies a small office on the third floor of an old building. There is no lift in the building and so employees have to walk up and down the stairs, often carrying heavy files containing clients' accounts.

The building doesn't have air conditioning, and the windows have bars on and can only open a small way. There is only one toilet and, because of the very old plumbing, it is often blocked and comes close to overflowing. There is a staff kitchen, which is small but clean. The kitchen only has a couple of electricity sockets, and these are often overloaded with plug adaptors. Many of Jones & Mooring's staff have worked in the building for a long time and they have grown to accept the problems.

1 Make a list of the potential hazards faced by staff at Jones & Mooring Partnership.

2 What should Jones & Mooring Partnership do to resolve these problems?

Activity: Health and safety risks

Identify the health and safety risks in the pictures below.

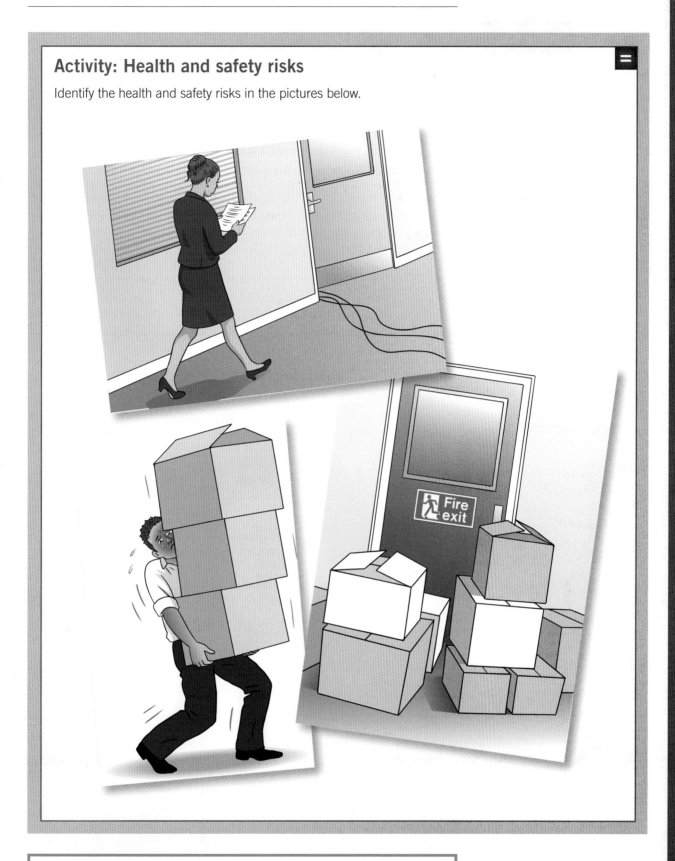

Just checking

1   What does the term health and safety mean?

2   Whose responsibility is it to make sure the working environment is healthy and safe?

3   What should you do if you see a risk to health and safety?

Maintaining safe and effective working practices

Every employee has a responsibility to maintain healthy and safe practices in the workplace. If you see something that is unsafe, such as a blocked fire escape, it is your responsibility to report the issue to your manager.

One part of maintaining health and safety is to keep your work area clean and tidy. Keeping your work area tidy will reduce the health and safety risks from, for example, boxes of papers blocking walkways, or dangling cables that could trip someone up. It will also help to promote more **effective working practices**.

While it may not feel like an important part of your job, keeping tidy will help you to be more effective. If your working area is untidy, it becomes more difficult for you to keep track of any important documents you may need to use. It also gives the impression that you are disorganised. This may affect how your colleagues perceive you.

Sian Parkin, AAT student member

Maintaining health and safety at work is everyone's responsibility.

Case study

That's not my job!

Jamie Jones is a trainee at an accountancy organisation. Jamie's responsibility is to prepare basic accounting records using a computerised accounting system.

When Jamie started his job, he was given health and safety training as part of his **induction**. However, he didn't pay much attention to the lessons on health and safety, and he didn't really remember what he was taught.

One Friday, Jamie arrived at work as usual and was astounded to find this memorandum on his desk.

Memo

To: Jamie Jones
From: Ian Smith
Date: 18/9/20XX
Subject: Health and safety problem

Please can you make sure that you tidy up after yourself. It has been noted that your work area on many occasions is surrounded by boxes that block the escape routes. Your desk is left untidy, with piles of paper, food and paper cups. It is organisational policy to maintain high standards of health, safety and cleanliness. Please can you rectify this situation as soon as possible.

Thank you.

Jamie is not very happy about this situation. The organisation employs cleaners and he thinks tidying up should be their job.

1 How is Jamie breaking the organisation's regulations?

2 If Jamie doesn't clear up his work area, what do you think Ian Smith might do?

3 Why are Jamie's actions inconsiderate and potentially dangerous to others?

Just checking

1 Who has responsibility for health and safety in the workplace?

2 Why is it important that fire exits are accessible at all times?

3 How might keeping a tidy desk help you in an accounting role?

When working in the accounting function of a business, you will have access to confidential personal information. In topic 2.1, we considered how to maintain confidentiality when working as an accounting professional. In this topic, we consider how to protect personal information.

Disclosing sensitive personal information without permission is a serious offence and may be illegal. You could be held personally liable for disclosing personal information without **authority**. Sensitive personal information could include details about the purchases made by a customer, as well as an individual's credit history, bank details, address and contact details. In the wrong hands, this information could be used for fraud or identify theft.

Worked example

Practical steps for maintaining the security of information

Figure 1.3 shows some of the procedures adopted by organisations for **securing** the confidential information that they hold.

Procedure for maintaining security	How this will help
Multi-level passwords on computer data	Multi-level passwords should restrict access so that employees only see what is relevant to their job role. This is not foolproof, but it reduces the chances of information being leaked or stolen.
Limit the number of people who can receive highly confidential information on paper	Restricts access to confidential information and, by keeping the number of copies to a minimum, reduces chances of security breaches.
Shred confidential papers	Shredding data after it is no longer needed improves security as the information can't be stolen or misused.
Lock filing cabinets and desk drawers	If cupboards or drawers that contain confidential information are kept locked, the data can't be removed by unauthorised employees.
Do not leave documents lying around	Anyone photocopying or faxing sensitive information should keep the documents with them at all times so that they are not left lying around the office where they can be read by unauthorised employees.

Figure 1.3: Procedures for maintaining the security of information

Activity: Security of electronic data

In this activity, focus on the practical steps you can take to keep information secure on a computer system. As an accounting professional, you will be working with information on computers on a daily basis. Think about steps you could take to avoid any data security problems.

1 Complete this mind map by adding extra branches. Two examples have been provided to help you get started.

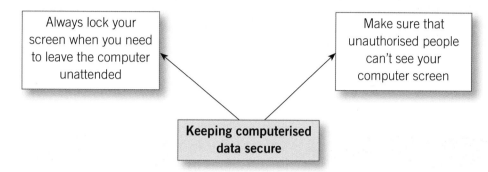

Always lock your screen when you need to leave the computer unattended

Make sure that unauthorised people can't see your computer screen

Keeping computerised data secure

2 Produce a guide that could be handed to accounting professionals to remind them of how to keep sensitive information secure. Provide examples of the practical measures they can take to maintain the security of electronic data.

Just checking

1 What kind of personal information might you be dealing with in an accountancy role?

2 What can you do to prevent paper-based information from being shared?

3 What can you do to prevent electronic information from being shared?

Efficient working practices

Efficiently: Completing work as quickly as possible to the required standards without making mistakes.

Time management: The process of organising your time so that tasks are completed by a given deadline.

Work plan: A list of jobs to complete, organised into the order in which they will be tackled and the time when each will be completed.

Organisations are very keen for their employees to work **efficiently**. This means getting a job done as quickly as possible, but with no mistakes and to a high standard. Tasks should be completed at a reasonable speed, but not rushed so that mistakes are made. By working in such a way, employees have a greater chance of achieving the goals they have been set.

As a professional working in an accounting function, you will be responsible for managing your own workload. You will have to think about **time management**. This involves organising your day so that tasks are completed on time. You may need to create **work plans**. These are simple documents that list all the jobs you have to do, estimate how long each is going to take to complete, and provide approximate times in the working day when you are going to complete each task.

When one person in a team has more work to complete than others, it may be necessary to share the work around. Managers often balance the workload across the whole team. This ensures that the team achieves all its work within the time available.

Case study

Jane Peel Accountancy

Jane Peel decided to set up her own accountancy business. Many businesses in her home town needed professional help to get their accounts in order. Jane's skills were highly sought after, as she had professional accounting qualifications and experience of working at a leading accountancy organisation. She managed to get many clients.

She was soon taking on more work than she could manage. Jane was a very thorough accountant and took great pains to make sure her work was error free, but she started to miss her clients' deadlines.

After six months, the work started to dry up. Jane started to worry, because she had quickly gone from having too much work to not having enough business to keep going. She phoned a few of her clients to find out why they had not sent her more business. She was surprised to learn that while customers were happy with the quality of her work, they weren't pleased about the missed deadlines.

1 What was Jane not doing properly?

2 Why were Jane's customers unhappy with her service?

3 What could Jane have done to be more efficient?

Activity: Creating a time plan

For this task, identify all the work you have to complete for the next month or so. This should include work for your AAT Access course, plus any other tasks at work, school or college, or in your personal life. Record the tasks in the first column of the table below, and then complete the other two columns for each task.

Task to be completed	Time it will take to complete the task	When the task needs to be completed

Now identify which tasks you need to do first if you are to complete them on time. This will help you prioritise your work.

Just checking

1 What does efficient mean?
2 Why do you have to be efficient in your learning, work and private life?
3 Why do accounting professionals have to be efficient?

✓
Homework

4.2 Communication within the team

When working as an accounting professional you are likely to be working as part of a team. While you will be working on your own individual tasks, you must remember that other members of your team will need your work to complete their tasks. For this reason, effective **communication** is important for the efficiency of the team.

There will be occasions when you have to advise your colleagues that you may not be able to make a deadline. You will need good communication skills to ask for help or to tell your colleagues to amend their work plans to accommodate the fact that your work will be late.

In a situation when you have to let people know that your work may be late, it is important to give your colleagues a revised date or time by which you will actually be able to complete the task. Your colleagues may then be able to create a **contingency** plan.

Case study

Team working

Sinead works in an accounting department with two other colleagues. She is responsible for gathering information, such as expenditure records, from the systems within the organisation. George takes this information and produces a profit and loss account for the organisation. Ahmed, who manages the accounting department, uses this profit and loss account to produce a quarterly report on the financial health of the organisation.

The accounting department has been very busy, and Sinead is running behind with her work. In order to produce the profit and loss account, George needs Sinead to hand over the income and expenditure records. Ahmed can't produce the financial report until he has the profit and loss account.

Sinead tells her colleagues that she will be able to produce the financial data a day later than planned. As George knows that the information will be coming to him a day later, he can complete the other work he has planned. This means that he can focus on producing the profit and loss account as soon as the information is available without getting behind with his work. This will mean that the profit and loss account will be available in good time for Ahmed to produce the financial report.

1 What might have happened if Sinead had not communicated the problem to her colleagues?

2 Why is it important for Sinead to know how long a task is going to take?

3 Why is it important that Sinead tells her colleagues when she will be able to produce the information?

Activity: Communication

Effective communication helps a team manage its work more efficiently. Link the scenarios below to the different communication methods listed opposite by choosing the best communication option in each instance.

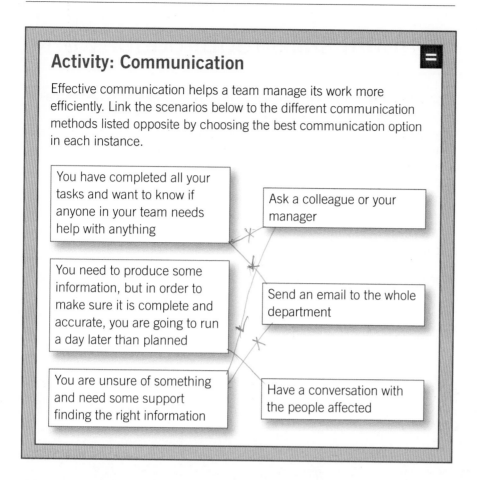

You have completed all your tasks and want to know if anyone in your team needs help with anything

You need to produce some information, but in order to make sure it is complete and accurate, you are going to run a day later than planned

You are unsure of something and need some support finding the right information

Ask a colleague or your manager

Send an email to the whole department

Have a conversation with the people affected

Just checking

1   Why is it important to keep colleagues informed of your progress on a task?

2   Why is it important to tell colleagues when you actually will be able to complete a task if you can't meet a deadline?

3   What is a contingency plan?

Homework

Personal skills required for work

When you are working as an accounting professional, your employer will have expectations that you need to fulfil. These expectations will range from general attributes, such as being reliable, to more job-specific skills, such as technical competence.

Important personal skills required by accounting professionals include good levels of numeracy and literacy, **integrity,** and an ability to work with computerised systems. Your employer will expect you to show a willingness to take on extra duties and to act in a professional manner at all times. Employers will also expect you to demonstrate a well-organised approach to your work.

Professionalism and integrity are two important qualities for anyone working in the accounting function. This is because the accounting profession relies heavily on its reputation for honesty and accuracy. As an accounting professional, you will be required to maintain high **standards** in your work.

Mark Wong, MAAT

Employers will expect you to have a range of personal skills, such as the ability to work in a team and to be punctual, as well as professional skills.

Worked example

Personal and professional skills

There is a range of professional skills, attributes and behaviours that employers expect from employees in the accounting profession. These are some of the key skills and attributes that employers will expect.

Professional skills	Personal attributes
Numeracy	Reliable
Good communication skills	Punctual
	Willing to learn
	Professional
	Well-organised

An employer may expect employees to be technically competent in the use of specific software or equipment. However, you may be provided with training to help you learn these skills. You should keep in mind that having the right attitude can go a long way towards getting the job you want.

Activity: Personal and professional skills

Visit a recruitment website on the internet and find a job advert for a junior accountancy role. Try to match the skills and personal attributes listed in the job advert to those listed in the table above. Where possible, give examples of how each skill or attribute listed in the advert might be used in the job role.

Just checking

1 Why might employers expect you to be willing to learn?

2 How many of the key professional skills and personal attributes do you think you currently have?

3 What do you think you can do to improve your skills and attributes? Focus on the areas where you think you lack the necessary skills.

How new skills and knowledge can be acquired

Key terms

Work shadowing: The process of following a more experienced member of staff around so that the junior member of staff picks up skills and ideas on how to do their own job more successfully.

Professional journals: Typically magazine-style publications written specifically for professionals in accounting positions. Journals contain information on significant changes in the accounting world, along with practical advice on how to complete particular tasks efficiently.

When working as an accounting professional it is important that you keep up to date with the requirements of the profession. This will require learning new skills and gaining further knowledge.

The world of accountancy is ever changing. You can only complete your job accurately and efficiently if you have the right skills. As an accounting professional, you will be expected as a matter of course to keep up to date with changes in the profession. An employee who is not willing to change is generally not going to succeed in accountancy.

You may improve your skills and knowledge by working alongside a more experienced colleague, who can show you how things should be done. Sometimes employers will use **work shadowing**. This is where you accompany a more experienced member of staff for a period to learn about a role or how the organisation works. You may be sent on day release to college or be given time within the working day to train and develop your skills.

You may also want to undertake some additional informal training through reading **professional journals**, books or using the internet. As a student member of the AAT, you will find a wide range of useful information at **aat.org.uk/members/**

It is important to make the most of any training opportunities you are offered, as they will help your professional development.

Case study

Pattison Accountants

Mary Smith has recently been employed as a trainee accounting technician with Pattison Accountants. The organisation has an excellent reputation for providing first-class training for new employees. It provides:

- a period of work shadowing
- AAT training with the local college
- a "buddy", a more experienced employee, who can advise and help with any problems the trainee may have.

1 Why would work shadowing help new employees?

2 How would having AAT-qualified staff help Pattison Accountants?

3 How does a work "buddy" help new employees?

Activity: Types of training

Job training can either be:

- formal – in which case you will receive tuition and it may lead to a qualification, such as AAT Access
- informal – in which case training is not structured or assessed.

Identify as many different types of formal and informal training as you can.

Formal training	Informal training

Just checking

1 What is a professional journal?

2 Give one example of off-the-job training.

3 What are the benefits to an employer of providing training for employees?

Setting goals for the acquisition of new skills

Key term

SMART target: A target that is specific, measurable, achievable, realistic and timed.

When working as an accounting professional, it is important that you set yourself learning goals that will help you develop professionally and that will support the goals of your employer. However, it is important that you set these goals with the support and guidance of your manager.

For example, you decide to set yourself a target to pass your AAT exams within the next 12 months. This is a **SMART target**, as it is:

- **S**pecific (pass exams)
- **M**easurable (you will either pass or fail exams)
- **A**chievable (giving yourself 12 months to do the work to pass exams)
- **R**ealistic (in terms of how much work you have to do), and
- **T**imed (pass within 12 months).

If targets are not SMART, then they are usually not very good targets.

Case study

Skills audit

In the early stage of your career, your employer will expect you to have the basic skills and attributes that all accounting professionals require.

Using the table below to undertake a skills audit, review how confident you feel about each skill or attribute listed in the table. You can use this exercise to set targets for development.

Professional skills	Tick the box that you feel applies best to you				
	1 Highly confident	2 Confident	3 About average	4 Unsure	5 Very unsure
Numeracy					
Communication skills					
Reliability					
Punctuality					
Willingness to learn					
Organisation					

This is just a snapshot of how you feel at present. However, it can be used to measure your progress, as you can compare how you have improved by completing the test again, say, in three months' time.

Activity: Setting SMART targets

Using the results of your skills audit, pick one area you want to improve. You need to think about how you will measure your improvement in this skill. For example, if you want to improve your punctuality, your goal might be to be on time for all deadlines and meetings.

Use the table below to help you write a SMART target for your improvement in this area.

		For example
Specific What do you want to achieve?		Pass AAT Access
Measurable How will you measure your success?		Achieve a Pass
Achievable		✓
Realistic		✓
Timed By when do you want to achieve this?		By September next year
SMART target		To pass AAT Access by September next year

Just checking

1 Who do you need to agree your training goals with?

2 Why is it important to set SMART targets?

3 Why is it important to review how you have achieved your training goals?

Check your understanding

Before you start this test of your knowledge and understanding, review the statements in the "Before you start" feature on page 9 and decide how confident you feel about the topics covered in this unit.

1 Which one of the following describes a private sector organisation?

    (a) An organisation set up to make a profit

    b An organisation paid for by taxes and providing essential services

    c An organisation set up to raise money for a cause

2 What is a public sector organisation set up to do?

    (a) Provide essential services and good value for money

    b Make a profit for its owners

    c Raise awareness and funds for a particular cause

3 Place a tick ✔ in the appropriate boxes to indicate which of these are internal customers of a business.

Suppliers	✓
Managers	
Customers	✓
Workers	✓
HM Revenue & Customs (HMRC)	

4 Which of the following functions is an accounts department most likely to deal with?

    a Selling goods to customers

    (b) Preparing profit and loss accounts

    c Creating marketing literature

    d Invoicing customers

5 Which of the following techniques would you **not** use to keep a sensitive electronic file secure and confidential?

    a Lock your computer screen whenever you are away from your desk

    b Use passwords to limit access to the file

    (c) Print out a copy to leave on your desk

    d Avoid letting anyone behind you see your screen unless it is absolutely necessary

6   Fill in the missing words.

When working in accounting, it is important that your work is
accurate so that it doesn't contain any errors. It is also important
that your work is *complete* so that your customers have all
the information they need. You should also make sure your work is
timely so it is ready for when your customers need it. However,
if you are running late, you need to *communicate* with anyone affected
so they can develop a contingency plan.

Words: timely, accurate, communicate, complete

7   Tick the two items from the list below that relate to learning new skills.

a   Application

b   Professional journal

c   Interview

d   Work shadowing

8   In a business, whose responsibility is maintaining healthy and safe
working practices?

a   Your employer's

b   Yours

c   Everyone's

d   The government's

9   If you find that you will be unable to complete your work in time for
a deadline, what should you do?

a   Not worry, everyone has got plenty of work

b   Let anyone affected know so they can adjust their plans

c   Focus on other less urgent tasks

d   Leave it until the last minute before telling your colleagues

10   What does being ethical when working in the accounting function mean?

a   Being honest and acting with integrity

b   Trying not to share too much private information with other people

c   Tidying up after yourself

d   Not sharing any information under any circumstances

Unit 2: Creating business documents

Introduction

Creating business documents is an essential skill for anyone working in an accounting function. Accounting professionals communicate regularly with their customers, and you will need to produce documents that create a positive and professional impression. To do this, you will need to make effective use of your time, keep high standards and check your work thoroughly. These essential skills are highly valued in the workplace.

By the end of this unit you will:

- know that there are different types of business document
- know why it is important to use the right communication style in business documents
- be able to produce routine business documents.

Zeya Phillips, Member in practice of Phillips Accountancy & Books

Creating business documents may not be much like making music, but it's important to strike the right note.

Before you start

Read the statements below and decide how much you agree with them.

	Agree	Not sure	Disagree
I know the different types of document I will be expected to use.			
I understand when to use each type of business document.			
I understand the difference between formal and informal communication.			
I know how to produce standard business documents.			
I understand why it's important to check documents for errors.			

1.1 Types of business document

When working in an accounting function you will use several different types of business document to **communicate** with **internal** and **external** **customers**. You will be expected to know the right **document** to use in any given situation. You should also be able to produce standard business documents.

An understanding of business documentation will enable you to communicate effectively within your workplace and to deal **professionally** with people from outside the organisation.

Worked example

Use of documents

Figure 2.1 shows the most common types of business document that you will use at work. These are letters, memos, emails and reports. You will use these documents for different situations.

- You will use letters to communicate with external customers of the organisation.
- You will use memos to communicate with staff inside the organisation.
- You will use emails for both internal and external communications.
- You will use reports to bring together information that the organisation has researched and compiled – both internal and external customers can use them.

Each type of document has a standard structure. For example, reports are usually organised into three main parts: introduction, main content, and conclusions and recommendations.

Letter

```
                                    Samuel Motors
                                    Back Henry Street
                                    Thornbury
                                    FY7 1XY

S Robinson
Ashdown Tyres
Flyde Road
Mythop FY6 2DP
                                    6 July 20XX

Dear Sandra

Ref: Cheque for £35.00 for invoice 236

Many thanks for your cheque, which we received this
morning.
```

Memo

```
                    Memo
To:       John Smith
From:     Abdul Mehmet
Date:     10 August 20XX
Subject:  Excel training

Please remind your staff that this is taking place at
10.30 in the ground floor training room.
```

Report

```
            Report
        Accounts 20XX–YY


        Prepared for:
        Samuel Motors

        Prepared by:
        JCS Accountancy
```

Email

```
From:     abc@abc.net
To:
Cc:
Subject:  Invoice number 134

Invoice number 134 is now overdue, please pay within 7 days to avoid late payment costs.
```

Figure 2.1: Types of business document

Activity: Business documents

1 Complete the table by giving an example of when you might use each of these documents.

Letter	
Memo	
Email	
Report	

Just checking

1 Why is it important to know which type of document to use in a given situation?
2 What type of documents is an organisation most likely to send to external customers?
3 What type of documents are external customers most likely to send to an organisation?

Homework

Templates

Templates are outline documents that allow business communications to be produced quickly and easily in a **consistent** style. When you receive a letter from your bank, for example, it will be based on the bank's letter template.

A letter template allows anyone within an organisation to create a letter that exactly matches the style of presentation that the organisation wants for its letters. This means that all letters sent by the organisation will look similar.

When working in an accountancy role, you will use a range of templates to save you time and to ensure that you present a consistent image of your organisation. In order to use templates effectively, you will need to have good computer skills.

Worked example

Letter templates

Imagine you work as an accounting technician for a major accountancy practice. Your daily work routine might involve regular contacts with customers. Very often, you may have to send similar communications to several customers. For example, you might need to send customers statements of their accounts on a regular basis.

Creating a letter from scratch every time you want to contact a customer would not be an effective use of your time. This is where templates can help you.

Figure 2.2 is an example of a template for one type of standard letter that an organisation might send out. The parts in grey show where the document can be customised to suit the requirements of a specific communication.

Apart from saving time, templates can also reduce the amount of errors that might occur in documentation. Since only a small amount of information needs to change each time a letter is sent to a customer, there are fewer opportunities to make mistakes.

 **Cash & Co Accountants**

<SENDERS NAME HERE>
<ADDRESS>
<ADDRESS>
<ADDRESS>

<INDIVIDUAL>
<COMPANY NAME IN FULL>
<ADDRESS>
<ADDRESS>
<ADDRESS>
<ADDRESS>

Highlighted parts of the letter can be edited

<DATE>

Dear <Mr or Mrs>

[<Ref: Job numbers/Supplier references>]

We are writing to you to complain about your invoice number [<number>] for £<amount of invoice> relating to the above <work or project>. Your original <estimate or quotation> dated [<Date>] was for £[<Insert Amount>] which was a fixed price for the work to be carried out. This was the basis upon which we entered into a contract with you.

You claim the increase is due to [<Describe>]. We have to inform you that this has no bearing on our contract. We at no time agreed with you that we would bear any additional costs due to [<eg external factors>] Our contractual obligation is therefore only to the original price shown in your <estimate quotations>.

Please find enclosed a cheque for the full payment of £[<Insert Amount>], in full and final settlement.

Yours sincerely

<Name>

Enc. cheque

Figure 2.2: Example of a letter template

Activity: Benefits of templates

Templates can help organisations in a number of different ways. Decide whether the statements below are true or false.

1 You can use templates to give a consistent, positive message to customers.
☑ True ☐ False

2 Templates mean that employees spend more time creating documents.
☐ True ☑ False

3 Templates need to be adapted each time before they are sent to customers.
☑ True ☐ False

4 Templates are only available for letters.
☐ True ☑ False

Just checking

Homework

1 What is a template?

2 How do templates help save time?

3 Apart from saving time, what other benefits do templates provide?

2.1 Formal and informal communication styles

As a general rule, **formal** communication is structured and professional. You will need to use a formal communication style most, if not all, of the time when producing documents in an accounting role. For example, you will use a formal communication style to write a business letter to an external customer. Formal communication won't include any **slang** and will rarely include **abbreviated language**.

Informal communication, on the other hand, is closer to how you might talk to your friends. It may be appropriate to use informal language in an email to a **peer** who works in the same organisation as you. However, you need to be careful not to use informal language in an official document meant for external customers as it will make you look unprofessional.

Each organisation will have its own rules about when it is appropriate to use informal communication. Unless it is explicitly stated, you should assume that you need to use formal communication.

Some communication methods are more formal than others. A business letter is a formal communication method, while an email or a memo may be more informal.

Worked example

Formal communication

Figure 2.3 is a formal letter. You will notice that the structure of the document and the way the message is presented is very different from how you might address someone you know well. Remember that when working as an accounting professional it is important that you give a professional impression. Customers will need to trust you with sensitive information, so being over-familiar may give them cause for concern.

Dear Ms Spencer

Please find enclosed the information requested during our telephone conversation of 14 February 20XX. As we discussed, I cannot supply the profit and loss accounts you request as the information you have submitted is incomplete.

As discussed, I will need the documents before I proceed, ideally within the next seven days, to ensure your accounts can be processed within the required timescale.

In the event that you require further assistance, please contact me on 01247 984560 during office hours.

Yours sincerely

Henry Jones
Accounts Assistant

Figure 2.3: A formal letter

Activity: Formal or informal?

Some communication methods are more formal than others. Rank the communication methods below from 1 (most formal) to 4 (most informal).

Memo or email

Phone call

Letter

Text message

Choose the best written communication method to use for each of the following.

1 Sending an external customer a reminder of outstanding payments.

2 Requesting further information from an external customer within the next two days.

3 Asking a colleague to send you a copy of a report that you need to consult.

Just checking

1 Why do accounting professionals use formal language?

2 Why is informal language inappropriate to use in a letter?

3 When might it be appropriate to use informal communication?

4 When ending a letter with your name, what other information should you give?

Key term

House style: A set of guidelines that state how to organise and present documents.

A **house style** is a set of rules and guidelines for presenting documents and information. Many organisations have their own house styles. This helps them to produce information in a consistent manner and gives customers a consistent experience of the organisation.

A house style gives employees clear rules for all aspects of a document, such as where logos should appear, what font to use, and what date format should be used. House styles are used to set up document templates, which save employees time when they need to create a standard letter, memo, invoice, and so on.

Worked example

Using a house style

House styles usually state where common elements of documents should be used. A house style may also state which font should be used in communications. A house style can be used across a range of common business documents. Figures 2.4 and 2.5 show a letter and an invoice that have been produced using the same house style.

Banbury Builders
34–39 Business Park
Banbury
Oxfordshire
OX16 6ZX

15 October 20XX

Dear Mr Green

Please find enclosed an invoice for the work completed by Brakes Solicitors. We look forward to receiving payment within the next 30 days.

Yours sincerely

Tariq Ashad
Accounts Assistant

Figure 2.4: A letter sent out to Banbury Builders using Brakes Solicitors' house style

Brakes Solicitors

Banbury Builders
34–39 Business Park
Banbury
Oxfordshire
OX16 6ZX

15 October 20XX

INVOICE 15 October 20XX

Legal advice: 3 hours @ £100 per hour	£300.00
Memorandum of advice: £75	£75.00
Total services:	£375.00
VAT (@ 20%):	£75.00
TOTAL DUE:	**£450.00**

Please forward payment within 30 days of the date on this invoice.

Figure 2.5: An invoice set out using Brakes Solicitors' house style

Activity: Identifying house style

Find several documents that you have received from one organisation. These might be communications from your bank, your phone provider or your local council. You could even use the documents that you have received from your training provider after enrolling on this course.

Look through the documents and try to identify the elements that have been set as house style. Remember that these will be features that are consistent across all the documents. Annotate the documents to show the house style.

1 As a customer, how does this use of house style affect you?

2 What are the benefits to the organisation of using a house style in this way?

Gethin Phillips, FMAAT

A house style will help an organisation present a consistent and professional image – and will save you time.

Just checking

1 What is a house style?

2 When might someone in a finance role use a house style?

3 Why might an organisation decide to use a house style?

Producing routine business documents

As an accounting professional, part of your normal **routine** will be to create and handle letters, memos, emails and reports. The purpose of these documents is usually to provide advice or request information. It is important to remember that someone reading the documents may be very busy, so every communication needs to be clear, well structured and to the point.

There are certain rules that you should follow when writing business communications. Some of these rules may seem obvious, but if they are ignored, letters, emails, memos and reports may look unprofessional. This may reflect badly both on your organisation and on your work.

It is important that you use **appropriate** language. For example, when writing a formal business letter, you will start with a greeting such as "Dear Mrs James". When signing a letter addressed to a named individual, you should end the communication with "Yours sincerely" followed by your name and your job title. If you don't know the name of the individual, the **opening salutation** may be "Dear Sir/Madam" and the **closing salutation** will be "Yours faithfully" followed by your name and your job title.

In emails, you can use more informal greetings and salutations. If you know the person you are sending the email to, you might use their first name and start with a greeting such as "Hello Diane". When ending an email, use "Regards" or "Kind regards" followed by your name and job title.

Worked example

Routine business documents

Business documents should follow a standard structure. A document should have an introduction that sets out its purpose, then cover the important information and main content, and finish with a closing sentence or some conclusions and recommendations. Your organisation may use document templates that include some of these elements. Figures 2.6, 2.7 and 2.8 show the standard structure of a letter, a memo and an email respectively.

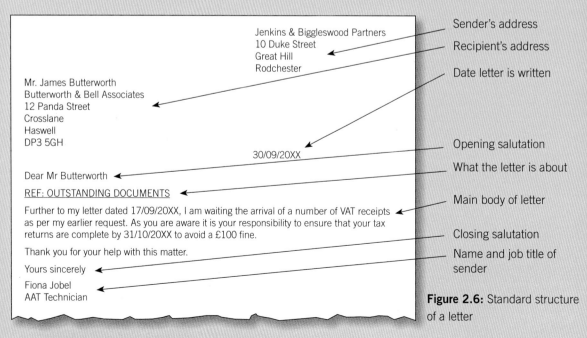

Jenkins & Biggleswood Partners
10 Duke Street
Great Hill
Rodchester

Mr. James Butterworth
Butterworth & Bell Associates
12 Panda Street
Crosslane
Haswell
DP3 5GH

30/09/20XX

Dear Mr Butterworth

REF: OUTSTANDING DOCUMENTS

Further to my letter dated 17/09/20XX, I am waiting the arrival of a number of VAT receipts as per my earlier request. As you are aware it is your responsibility to ensure that your tax returns are complete by 31/10/20XX to avoid a £100 fine.

Thank you for your help with this matter.

Yours sincerely

Fiona Jobel
AAT Technician

- Sender's address
- Recipient's address
- Date letter is written
- Opening salutation
- What the letter is about
- Main body of letter
- Closing salutation
- Name and job title of sender

Figure 2.6: Standard structure of a letter

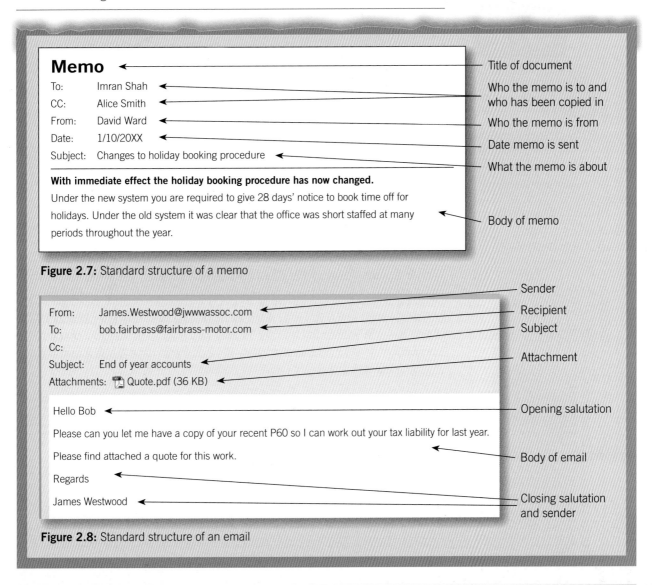

Figure 2.7: Standard structure of a memo

Figure 2.8: Standard structure of an email

Activity: Creating documents

You need to request further information from Jane Smith for the end of year accounts. You will need her to supply you with the expenses details for the period 01.06.20XX to 30.06.20XX by next Tuesday.

Create an email to request this information. Make sure you that your document includes:

- an appropriate subject
- an introduction to the communication
- a suitable closing sentence

- an appropriate greeting and salutation
- the key information that you need
- a closing salutation.

Now identify which other communication methods could have been used for the same message.

When completing this activity, you may find it useful to refer back to the sections on using templates and formal and informal communication styles (pages 44–47).

Just checking

1 If you open a letter with "Dear Mr Pathetis", how would you end the letter?

2 If you end a letter with "Yours faithfully", do you know the addressee's name?

3 Why is it important to remember to include the subject of the communication?

3.2 Checking documents for accuracy

Key terms

Accurate: The ability to complete and review work without making mistakes.

Numerate: Being skilled at dealing with numbers.

Literate: Being skilled at dealing with written content.

When working as an accounting professional, you will be expected to demonstrate a high level of accuracy in your work. In a busy accounting environment, you will need to work quickly and effectively while producing **accurate** documents. For this, you need to have good **numeracy** and **literacy** skills.

Whatever type of document you are working on, there are two key aspects that you will need to check for accuracy.

- Spelling and grammar – if your documents include spelling mistakes and poor grammar, they will look unprofessional and give customers a bad impression of you and your organisation.

- Factual accuracy – you may need to include figures, reference numbers and dates in your communications. It is very important that you check these carefully, as it won't be immediately obvious if you have made a mistake in keying them in.

Case study

Kelly, Warrington & Partners

Kelly, Warrington & Partners is a small accountancy firm. It has had a very busy few months, and so the partners have employed Shaun to help them get up to date with the administrative work. However, the partners are concerned that Shaun is introducing errors into their work.

Your manager has asked you to check some of Shaun's work. Figure 2.9 shows an email that one of the partners had sent Shaun. Figure 2.10 shows the letter that Shaun has produced.

1 Check the letter for spelling and grammar.

2 Check the letter for factual accuracy.

3 Is there anything else you feel should be corrected?

Date:	Wed, 12 October 20XX
To:	Shaun <shaun@kwaccounts.co.uk>
From:	James Kelly <james.kelly@kw.accounts.co.uk>
Subject:	West Coast Tearooms Account HJF013

Hello Shaun

Please could you prepare a letter and an invoice to Sally Thorpe at West Coast Tearooms, Royal Albert Drive, Scarborough, advising her that we have completed their accounts for 20XX. The work took 8 hours, and we agreed an hourly rate with them of £75.00 plus VAT at 20%. Remind the client that payment is due within 30 days. Please pass the letter for signature before sending to the client.

Regards

James

James Kelly
Senior Partner
Kelly, Warrington & Partners
The High
York

Figure 2.9: The email sent to Shaun

Kelly, Warrington & Partners

West Coast Tearooms
Royal Albert Drive
Scarborough

Kelly, Warrington & Partners
The High
York

12 October 20XX

Dear Ms Thrope

Re. West Coast Teamrooms Account HKF013

We have now completed the accounts for 20XX. Please find enclosed an invoice for the work as follows.

Compiling accounts: 8 hours @ £75.00	£600.00
VAT (@20%)	£120.00
Total due:	£720.00

Please forward payment to us within 30 days.

Yours faithfully

James Kelly
Senior Partner

Figure 2.10: The letter produced by Shaun

Just checking

1 What does accuracy mean?

2 Why would an employer expect you to be numerate and literate?

3 What type of mistakes do you think you will find most frequently in letters when working in an accounts department?

Check your understanding

Before you start this test of your knowledge and understanding, review the statements in the "Before you start" feature on page 41 and decide how confident you feel about the topics covered in this unit.

1 Which of the following documents would be most appropriate to inform staff of a change in procedures at your office?

  a Report

  b Letter

  c Memo

2 Why are templates helpful to an accounting organisation? Tick the two correct answers.

  a They never need to be changed.

  b They reduce errors.

  c They save time.

  d They mean you don't need to use a computer.

3 Match the following words to the terms in the table.

Formal   Informal

Less structured and conventional language and communication	
Language and communication following standard rules and conventions	

4 Which would be the most appropriate communication style to use if you are writing to someone who you had met before but did not know well?

  a Conversational

  b Formal

  c Informal

5 How should a formal letter always start?

  a Hiya

  b Dear

  c Hello

6 What should the cover of a report contain?

  a A list of the tables in the report

  b Who the report is for and who it is written by

  c Yesterday's date

7 What should an email always contain?

  a Subject

  b An accounting reference number

  c Personal conversations

8　Match the following words to the terms in the table.

　　Literate　　　　Numerate　　　　Accuracy

Being skilled at dealing with written content	
The ability to complete and review work without making mistakes	
Being skilled at dealing with numbers	

9　What is the purpose of a report?

　a　To improve the presentation of documents

　b　To bring together information that has been researched and compiled

　c　To send to customers

10　How would you end a formal communication to Mr Disraeli?

　a　Yours faithfully

　b　Thanks

　c　Yours sincerely

11　Which of the following would not be included in a report?

　a　Introduction

　b　Main content

　c　Conclusions

　d　Closing salutation

Unit 3:
Essential accounting procedures

Introduction

All organisations have to keep accurate financial records, so it is important that they have systems in place to help them do this. When you are working in a finance role, you will have to follow these systems to make sure records are accurate and up to date. As well as following the procedures, you will also need to be familiar with the accounting terminology used in the business world.

By the end of this unit you will:

- understand basic accounting terminology
- understand the use of business documents
- prepare to record business transactions in the books of prime entry
- understand types of coding and batch control
- be able to prepare documents to process receipts and payments
- be able to prepare a basic profit statement.

Robin Meynell, FMAAT

Accountants need to follow set procedures. Just like playing pool, working in finance means you have to know and understand the sequence in which everything should happen.

Before you start

Read the statements below and decide how much you agree with them.

	Agree	Not sure	Disagree
I understand basic accounting terminology.			
I am able to use examples to support my understanding of basic accounting terminology.			
I can identify the documents used in buying and selling goods on credit.			
I can identify the documents used in buying and selling goods for cash.			
I know which business transactions are recorded in each book of prime entry.			
I understand types of coding and batch control.			
I know how to process receipts.			
I know how to process payments.			
I understand the difference between gross profit and net profit.			
I know how to prepare a basic profit statement.			

Assets and liabilities

Key terms

Assets: Items of value owned by an organisation.

Liability: Money owed by an organisation to other organisations, businesses and individuals.

Overdraft: An arrangement that allows an organisation to take more money out of its bank account than it has on deposit.

Bank loan: A fixed amount of money an organisation borrows from a bank.

Debtor: A person or business that owes money to an organisation. A debtor is an asset because the money belongs to the organisation even though it has not actually received it yet.

Creditor: A person or business to whom an organisation owes money. A creditor is a liability because the money belongs to another person or business.

All organisations, however big or small, own items of value. These could be anything from a bucket and ladder for a window cleaner to a jumbo jet for an airline. Items of value owned by an organisation are called **assets**. The assets of most organisations are likely to include premises, vehicles and machinery, as well as stock and cash.

Organisations also usually owe some money to other organisations. Anything owed by an organisation is called a **liability**. The liabilities of an organisation might include an **overdraft** or **bank loan**, as well as money owed to suppliers.

At work, you may be responsible for keeping a record of your organisation's assets and liabilities. One of the assets might be **debtors**. These are people who owe your organisation money. Your job might involve identifying when money is overdue, and writing to or ringing up a customer to ask for payment. Your organisation might also owe money to other organisations: these are called **creditors**. Your job might involve ensuring that these organisations are paid on time. At the end of a year, the accountant will summarise these assets and liabilities.

Case study

Craig's Computer World

Craig runs a small but successful business supplying computer accessories and supplies to individuals and organisations across Lancashire. He has a small shop in Preston and also makes sales through a website.

Most of his customers pay cash, but he allows organisations to have 30 days to pay for their purchases. Craig imports most of his stock, such as CDs and keyboards, from abroad. His suppliers allow him 30 days to pay for his purchases.

Craig set up the business five years ago with a bank loan to help him buy the premises and a delivery van. The table on page 59 lists Craig's assets and liabilities.

Assets	
Premises The shop Craig sells his computer supplies from	Cash The money Craig has in his cash register and also in the bank
Vehicles A delivery van used to deliver larger orders to local organisations	Fixtures and fittings The shop fittings, such as shelves, display units and carpets
Equipment The items of equipment he uses to help run his business, such as a computer, printer and cash register	Stock All the items he has available to sell to his customers
Debtors The business customers that have made a purchase but have yet to pay for them – Craig gives business customers 30 days to pay for their purchases	
Liabilities	
Bank loan The money Craig still owes from borrowing from the bank	Creditors Money that Craig owes to his suppliers who have given him 30 days to pay for his purchases

1 With the use of an example, explain what the term asset means.

2 With the use of an example, explain what the term liability means.

3 Why are debtors classed as assets?

4 Why are creditors classed as liabilities?

Activity: Identifying assets and liabilities

In this activity you are going to practise applying the terms you have learnt to an organisation you are familiar with.

Think of an organisation that you know quite well. This may be a workplace, a leisure facility or somewhere you visit regularly. Write a list of all the assets that the organisation owns.

What liabilities might it have? Write a list. This may be more difficult as you can see the organisation's assets, but its liabilities may not be known to you.

Just checking

1 Describe an asset.

2 Describe a liability.

3 Is a debtor an asset or a liability?

4 Is an organisation's debt an asset or a liability?

Income and expenditure

Most organisations have money coming in and going out on a daily basis. This works in the same way as it does on a personal level. For example, you might receive money from a wage and then spend that money on food and other items. The money an organisation earns from selling goods and services to its customers is called **income**.

An organisation will also have expenses. It will spend money on items such as stock, electricity and wages. This is called **expenditure**.

At work you might be responsible for keeping a record of all the income and expenditure of an organisation. You will learn about how these are recorded on pages 74–79. At the end of the year the accountant will summarise all the income and expenditure.

Case study

Craig's Computer World

Craig keeps a record of all the sales he makes in order to be able to calculate his total income. At the end of each day, he adds up his sales to see what his income is for the day.

He also records all his expenditure, but he only adds this up once a month. This is because some of his expenses (such as wages) are paid monthly, and others (such as his gas and electricity bill) are only paid every three months.

Here is an example of Craig's income from his internet sales on 31 March.

Customer	Sales	Total
Mr Esmail	Blank CDs @ £15.99	£15.99
MPR Ltd	Mouse and keyboard @ £36.00 Printer @ £500.00 10 reams of paper @ £3.50 per ream 5 packs of inkjet labels @ £6.00 per pack	£36.00 £500.00 £35.00 £30.00
Susan Smith	Plastic wallets @ £8.50	£8.50
Total 31 March		**£625.49**

Craig has also made a list of all his items of expenditure:

Stock	Wages	Electricity
Fuel	Marketing	Van tax and MOT
Postage	Stationery	Miscellaneous

Web maintenance and hosting

1 How many customers did Craig have on his internet site on 31 March?

2 Where else may Craig have generated income on 31 March?

3 How much did MPR Ltd spend on 31 March?

4 With the use of an example, explain what is meant by income.

5 With the use of an example, explain what is meant by expenditure.

Activity: Examples of income and expenditure

In this activity you are going to practise applying the terms you have learnt to an organisation that you know well.

Think of an organisation you are familiar with, such as a workplace, a leisure facility or somewhere you visit regularly. You might want to use the same organisation that you investigated for the previous activity (see page 59).

Write down where your chosen organisation gets its income from. Write down all the expenses that you think it might have to pay.

Mathematics for accounting

Craig has started to record his sales for 1 April, but has not yet calculated his total income for the day. Complete the table to calculate Craig's income for 1 April.

Customer	Sales	Total
Kevin Barker	4 reams of printer paper @ £3.50 per ream	£14.00
Sharma Aresh	CDs @ £8.50	£8.50
Top Training Ltd	2 ink toners @ £75.00 per toner	£150.00
Mrs Gainsford	2 packs of CD labels @ £16.00 per pack	£32.00
Total 1 April		£204.50

Just checking

1 For an organisation, what does the term income mean?

2 For an organisation, what does the term expenditure mean?

3 Give two examples of income and two examples of expenditure for an organisation.

Hw

1.3 The sale and purchase of goods for cash and on credit

Key terms

Cash sale: The customer pays for goods or services at the time of the sale.

Credit sale: The customer is allowed to pay for the goods or services some time after the sale. The customer is now a debtor of the organisation.

Cash purchase: An organisation pays the supplier for items of expenditure at the time of purchase.

Credit purchase: An organisation pays the supplier for items of expenditure some time after making the purchase. The supplier is now a creditor of the organisation.

Income is the money coming into the organisation from sales. Sometimes, these will be **cash sales**. This means the customer pays at the time they receive the goods or service. On other occasions, the organisation may not ask the customer for immediate payment. These are known as **credit sales**.

The same is true of expenditure. The organisation may pay for the goods or service at the time it makes the purchases (these are **cash purchases**), or it may be able to pay later by buying on credit (these are **credit purchases**).

The type of sale or purchase affects the timing of the receipt of money or payment of money. Organisations may try to get their customers to make cash purchases or offer short credit terms. Credit terms are the length of time an organisation gives a customer to pay for a purchase. On the other hand, an organisation might try to avoid making cash purchases from its suppliers and might try to negotiate long credit terms. This will speed up the flow of money into the organisation but slow down the flow out.

Case study

Craig's Computer World

Craig has two types of customers: individuals and organisations. When selling to individuals (that is, the general public), he expects payment straight away. These are all cash sales. When selling to organisations, he allows his customers to pay 30 days after the sale. These are all credit sales. Remember:

Customer pays immediately = cash sale

Customer delays payment = credit sale

Craig pays for some of his expenses at the same time as he receives the goods or services. For example, he pays the window cleaner once a week immediately after having his windows cleaned. This is a cash purchase. When buying stock, his suppliers allow him up to 30 days to pay for the goods after he has received them. This is a credit purchase.

Craig pays immediately = cash purchase

Craig delays payment = credit purchase

1 Suppose Craig sells 1,000 CDs to an organisation called Branigans Bargains Ltd. He allows Branigans 30 days to pay. What is this an example of?
   a a credit purchase
   b a cash purchase
   c a credit sale
   d a cash sale

2 What term is used when a customer pays Craig for goods at the time of the sale? *a cash sale*

3 What term is used when Craig pays for his supplies some time after receiving them? *a credit purchase*

Activity: Terminology

Link the terms below that are associated with the sale and purchase of goods for cash or on credit with the correct description of the term.

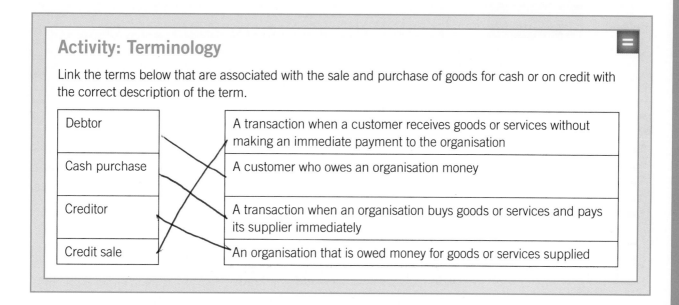

Debtor	A transaction when a customer receives goods or services without making an immediate payment to the organisation
Cash purchase	A customer who owes an organisation money
Creditor	A transaction when an organisation buys goods or services and pays its supplier immediately
Credit sale	An organisation that is owed money for goods or services supplied

Just checking

1 How is a cash transaction different from a credit transaction?

2 Why is it better for an organisation if customers pay by cash?

3 Why is it better for an organisation if it pays for goods and services on credit?

4 An organisation offers 60 days' credit to its customers. If a sale is made in March, when will the organisation receive the money for the sale?

1.4 Cash transactions and credit transactions

When an organisation makes a sale and receives immediate payment, this is called a **cash transaction**. The term cash transaction also applies when an organisation purchases goods or services and pays immediately. A **credit transaction** is when an organisation makes a sale and receives payment some time in the future. Similarly, when an organisation purchases goods or services on credit, this is also classed as a credit transaction.

Many small or new businesses only have cash transactions. For example, a market stall selling flowers is likely to buy its stock each morning in cash and then take cash payments from its customers. Larger and more established firms, however, are likely to make a combination of cash and credit sales, and they will buy many goods and services from their suppliers on credit terms.

Case study

The ice man

Tom runs a small fleet of ice cream vans. He buys ice cream in bulk from a food manufacturer that offers him 30 days' credit. He buys other supplies from a warehouse, and pays for these in cash. He pays casual workers on a daily basis to work on the vans at busy periods.

Tom's sales are only through the vans, and he only accepts immediate cash payments from his customers. This means that Tom has a combination of cash and credit transactions. These are summarised in the table.

Transactions	Cash transactions	Credit transactions
Purchase ice cream		✓
Purchase other supplies	✓	
Pay casual workers	✓	
Sales to customers	✓	

Indicate whether each of these statements is true or false.

a Tom pays for all his supplies immediately. F

b Tom makes cash and credit sales. F

c Tom makes cash and credit purchases. T

d Credit transactions are when all goods purchased have to be paid for before they are received. F

Activity: Cash and credit transactions

In this activity, you will practise applying the terms you have learnt to an organisation. Think of an organisation you know well, such as a workplace, a leisure facility or somewhere you visit regularly. This can be the organisation you have used for earlier activities in this unit.

1 Does it make cash sales and credit sales?
   a Cash sales: (Yes) / No
      If yes, provide an example.
   b Credit sales: Yes / (No)
      If yes, provide an example.

2 Does it make cash purchases and credit purchases?
   a Cash purchases: Yes / No
      If yes, provide an example.
   b Credit purchases: Yes / No
      If yes, provide an example.

3 Why do you think organisations use a combination of cash and credit transactions? Think through what this means to an organisation, such as the one you used for questions 1 and 2. Try to identify one advantage and one disadvantage of each type of transaction.

Mathematics for accounting

Jeremiah Fashions makes both cash sales and credit sales. For every £1,000 of sales, £250 are made in cash. What percentage of Jeremiah's sales are cash?

Just checking

1 Your organisation has sold 50 tickets to a charity dinner at £35 per ticket. You have sent the tickets to your customers and asked them to pay within 30 days. Are these sales an example of a cash transaction or a credit transaction?

2 The hotel hosting the charity dinner has asked you to pay a 30% deposit on the room, and the remainder on the day of the event. What is this an example of?
   a a cash transaction
   b a credit transaction
   c a cash and credit transaction

3 The band that will be entertaining your guests at the dinner want paying on the night. What is this an example of?
   a a cash transaction
   b a credit transaction
   c a cash and credit transaction

Profit and loss

Key terms

Profit: When an organisation earns more money than it spends.

Loss: When an organisation spends more money than it earns.

Gross profit: The profit from sales less the cost of sales.

Net profit: Gross profit less expenses, such as wages, electricity and marketing costs.

Sales income: The money coming into an organisation from sales of goods and services. For a single product, income can be calculated by multiplying the number of items sold by the price of the item.

Making a **profit** is a key target for a business such as a limited company. If an organisation makes a profit, it means that it has received more money (income) than it has spent (expenditure). However, if an organisation spends more than it earns, it has made a **loss**. Many new businesses go through an initial period of making a loss. If they continue to lose money, they may be shut down.

For this course, you need to understand that there are two different types of profit: **gross profit** and **net profit**.

Worked example

Gross profit and net profit

Gross profit is worked out by subtracting the cost of sales from the **sales income**.

| **Sales income**
Sum of all money coming into the organisation from sales for the chosen period. | minus | **Cost of sales**
Sum of money spent in making those sales, such as purchasing stock. |

Gross profit
If the figure is positive (more than 0), the organisation has made a gross profit. If it is negative, the organisation has made a loss.

However, the organisation spends more money than just the cost of sales. For example, the cost of sales will not include wages or any rent and rates the organisation pays on its property. The net profit is a more accurate measure of an organisation's profitability. It can be calculated by subtracting all the expenses of the organisation from the gross profit.

| Gross profit | minus | Expenses (such as wages, rent and rates) | | Net profit |

Figure 3.1: How to calculate gross profit and net profit

- If total income is greater than the cost of sales plus the expenses, then the organisation has made a profit.
- If total income is less than the cost of sales plus the expenses, then the organisation has made a loss.
- If total income is the same as the cost of sales plus the expenses, then the organisation has not made a profit or a loss.

Activity: Profit or loss?

1 What has an organisation with costs of sales plus expenses below total income made?

(a) a profit

b a loss

c neither a profit nor a loss

2 What has an organisation that has total income of £35,000 and costs of sales plus expenses of £33,000 made?

(a) a profit

b a loss

c neither a profit nor a loss

3 What has an organisation with total income lower than costs of sales plus expenses made?

a a profit

(b) a loss

c neither a profit nor a loss

4 What has an organisation with total income of £150,000 and costs of sales plus expenses of £150,000 made?

a a profit

b a loss

(c) neither a profit nor a loss

Mathematics for accounting

These are last month's expenditure and income figures for an organisation.

Expenditure	Income
Cost of sales: £1,137.49	Sales: £2,108.20
Rent: £275.00	
Staff wages: £507.20	
Gas and electricity: £69.32	

Work out whether the organisation made a net profit or loss for the month. See pages 96–97 if you are unsure of the mathematical skills you need to apply.

Just checking

1 If an organisation's income is more than its expenditure, is it in profit?

2 What is gross profit?

3 What is net profit?

Documents used in the process of buying and selling goods on credit

Key terms

Purchase order: A document sent to a supplier detailing the goods that the customer wants to purchase.

Invoice: A document sent by the supplier to the customer listing the goods supplied and requesting payment for these goods.

Credit note: A note informing the customer of any amounts refunded by the supplier following the return of goods or errors on a previous invoice. The credit note can be used against outstanding invoices.

Remittance advice: A document sent to inform the supplier that an invoice has been paid.

Statement of account: A document that summarises the transactions between a supplier and customer. It shows the invoices and credit notes sent, payments received and any outstanding balance on the account.

As part of the sales process, documents will be used to place the order (a **purchase order**), and request payment (an **invoice**). If the order is incorrect in some way or if the goods are returned to the supplier, a document (a **credit note**) will also be used to inform the customer that they will not be charged for these goods. Once the customer is satisfied with the delivery and they have received an invoice, they will send payment with a document called a **remittance advice**. This contains details of the invoice being paid.

You will use the same documents when making sales to customers and when buying goods and services from a supplier. When you place an order with one of your suppliers, you will send a purchase order, and the supplier will then send you the goods and an invoice requesting payment.

At the end of each month you will send each customer a **statement of account** that summarises all their transactions with your organisation for the month and shows whether any money is outstanding. At the same time, you can expect to receive a statement of account from your suppliers.

At work you might be asked to complete all these documents and to store them safely, so that your organisation has a record of its transactions.

Worked example

Recording a transaction

When an organisation buys or sells goods or services on credit, the documents that are exchanged provide a record of the transaction for both the supplier and the customer. They inform both parties of the stages being taken to process and complete the order.

Customer	⟹	Purchase order	⟹	Supplier
Customer	⟸	Invoice	⟸	Supplier
Customer	⟸	Statement of account	⟸	Supplier
Customer	⟹	Remittance advice	⟹	Supplier

Figure 3.2: The exchange of documents between customer and supplier

If there is a mistake made with the delivery, or if the customer returns all or part of the delivery, then the invoice will be incorrect. The invoice will be charging the customer for more goods than the customer has accepted. In these circumstances, the supplier will send a credit note to inform the customer of the correct amount to be paid.

| Customer | ⟸ | Credit note | ⟸ | Supplier |

Just checking

Read each of the following statements and use a tick ✔ to indicate whether they are true or false.

Statement	True	False
A purchase order is sent from a customer to a supplier	✓	
A remittance advice is sent before an invoice		✓
A statement of account is sent with every order		✓
An invoice is sent from a customer to a supplier		✓
A credit note may be sent from the supplier to the customer	✓	
A credit note is sent for all credit transactions		✓

Activity: The documents process

You are employed by Retro Bags as an accounts assistant with responsibility for accepting orders and ensuring all the relevant documents are completed and sent to customers. This is one of the purchase orders you have been passed.

Funky Fashions

10 Premier Road,
Selcroft, SE2 3TF   VAT registration no: 656 121236

Purchase order no: 361

To: Retro Bags   Date: 17 February 20XX
    62 West Parade, Selcroft, SE3 6HH

	£
20 bags (purple) @ £15.00	300.00
10 bags (small) @ £6.00	60.00
Sub total	360.00
VAT @ 20%	72.00
Total	432.00

Delivery instructions: asap

Use the information provided in the purchase order to complete the invoice. Date the invoice 20 February 20XX. This will help you to remember what information is shown on an invoice.

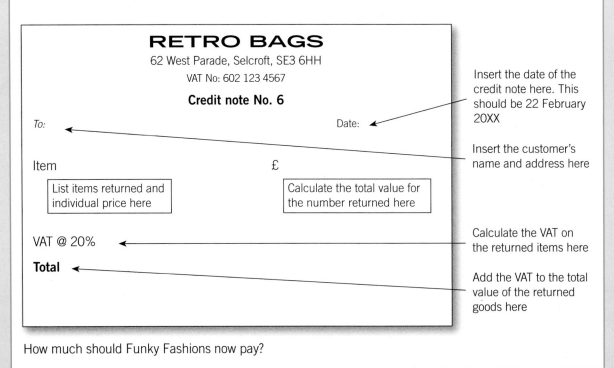

RETRO BAGS
62 West Parade, Selcroft, SE3 6HH

VAT No: 602 123 4567

Invoice No. 2719

To: Funky Fashions
    10 Premier Road, Selcroft, SE2 3TF

Date: ◄——

Insert the date of the invoice here. This should be 20 February 20XX

Item   £

| List items purchased and individual prices here | List total price for items here |

Sub total ◄——

Add up the cost of the order here

VAT @ 20% ◄——

Calculate the VAT here

Total ◄——

Add the VAT to the subtotal here

Terms: 30 days net

Two days later, a member of staff at Funky Fashions phones to say that the delivery was wrong and that they only received five small bags. You offer to send five more straight away, but Funky Fashions would rather be sent a credit note for the missing bags. Comply with this request by completing the credit note below. This will help you to remember what information is shown on a credit note.

RETRO BAGS
62 West Parade, Selcroft, SE3 6HH

VAT No: 602 123 4567

Credit note No. 6

To: ◄——

Date: ◄——

Insert the date of the credit note here. This should be 22 February 20XX

Insert the customer's name and address here

Item   £

| List items returned and individual price here | Calculate the total value for the number returned here |

VAT @ 20% ◄——

Calculate the VAT on the returned items here

Total ◄——

Add the VAT to the total value of the returned goods here

How much should Funky Fashions now pay?

It is now the end of the month (28 February 20XX) and the remittance for invoice 2719 has not yet been received. Complete the statement of account below.

RETRO BAGS
62 West Parade, Selcroft, SE3 6HH

Statement of account 21

To: Funky Fashions
10 Premier Road, Selcroft, SE2 3TF

Date: 28 -feb- 2014

	£
Balance brought forward as at 1 February	0.00
Invoice 2719	432.00
Credit note 6	36.00
Balance	396.00
Balance carried forward 28 February 20XX	£ 396.00

Insert the date of the statement of account. This is 28 February 20XX

Insert the value of the invoice and the credit note here. Remember that the credit note will be a minus value. Indicate this by putting brackets round the amount

Calculate the total balance by adding the positive numbers and subtracting the negative numbers (the numbers in brackets)

Just checking

Complete the following sentences by selecting the most appropriate option from this list:
- purchase order
- invoice
- credit note
- remittance advice
- statement of account

a An organisation sends a _Credit note_ to correct an invoice.

b A customer sends a _remittance advice_ to inform the supplier of payment.

c An organisation sends an _invoice_ to list items supplied and request payment.

d An organisation sends a _Statement of account_ to summarise transactions at the end of a month.

e A customer sends a _purchase order_ to tell a supplier what they want to purchase.

The documents organisations use to record cash transactions tend to be more straightforward than those used for credit transactions. The order will normally be made verbally and the payment is handed over straight away. There is therefore no need for a complex exchange of documents between the customer and the supplier.

If you deal directly with customers or suppliers, you may be involved with cash transactions. When an organisation pays a supplier in cash, or when a customer pays in cash, the person giving the money will want a **receipt** as proof that they have paid.

Worked example

Cash transactions

Cash transactions are very straightforward.

1 The customer places the order.

2 The supplier gives the goods.

3 The customer pays by cash.

4 The supplier gives a receipt.

No. _____	No. _____ Date: _____
From: _____	Received from: _____
_____	_____
Date: _____	The sum of _____
£ _____	_____
	£ _____ Signed: _____

Figure 3.3: An example of a receipt

The supplier who has received the cash will keep the receipt stub, and the customer paying the cash will get the main receipt.

Jennifer O'Hare, MAAT

When you buy small items such as a coffee or a paper, you will probably pay by cash and will receive a receipt to show you have paid for the goods.

Activity: Receipts

Link the type of information that needs to be recorded on a receipt to the terms listed below.

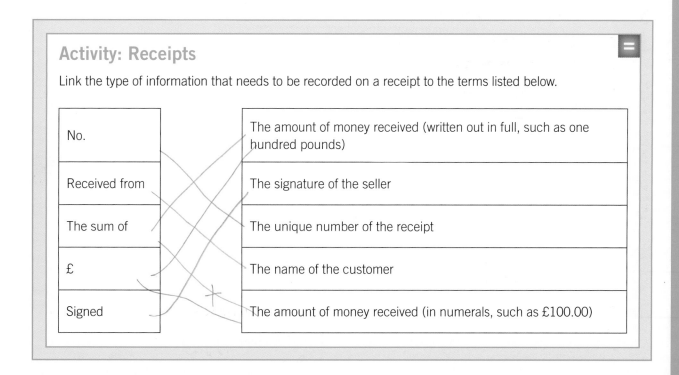

No.	The amount of money received (written out in full, such as one hundred pounds)
Received from	The signature of the seller
The sum of	The unique number of the receipt
£	The name of the customer
Signed	The amount of money received (in numerals, such as £100.00)

Just checking

Indicate whether each of these statements is true or false.

1 An organisation gives a receipt to a customer who has paid in cash. T
2 A supplier will send an invoice to a customer who pays in cash. F
3 A receipt is a method of payment for a cash transaction. F
4 A receipt is proof of payment. T

Key terms

Sales daybook: A record of all invoices sent out to customers.

Sales returns daybook: A record of all credit notes sent out to customers.

Cash receipts book: A record of all income received by an organisation.

Purchases daybook: A record of all invoices received from suppliers.

Purchases returns daybook: A record of all credit notes received from suppliers.

Cash payments book: A record of all an organisation's expenditure.

Every transaction made by an organisation has to be recorded. The first place it is recorded is called a book of prime entry. (Prime simply means first.) The type of transaction determines which book it is recorded in.

The books of prime entry used to record an organisation's sales are the **sales daybook**, the **sales returns daybook** and the **cash receipts book**.

The books of prime entry used to record an organisation's purchases are the **purchases daybook**, the **purchases returns daybook** and the **cash payments book**.

When working in an accounts office you will need to be able to take the information from documents such as invoices and credit notes and enter the details into the correct book of prime entry.

Worked example

Books of prime entry

As an organisation makes cash and credit transactions with customers and suppliers, information about these transactions will be recorded in one of the books of prime entry.

Transaction	Book of prime entry
Credit sale to a customer	Sales daybook
Goods returned from a customer	Sales returns daybook
Income received	Cash receipts book
Credit purchase from a supplier	Purchases daybook
Goods returned to a supplier	Purchases returns daybook
Expenses paid	Cash payments book

Activity: Match the transactions

Listed below are six transactions. Use a tick ✔ to allocate each transaction to one of the daybooks.

Transaction	Sales daybook	Sales returns daybook	Cash receipts book	Purchases daybook	Purchases returns daybook	Cash payments book
Cheque received from a customer			✓			
Cash sales for the day of £600			✓			
Goods returned from an unhappy customer		✓				
Faulty components sent back to a supplier					✓	
Cash payment to a supplier						✓
Wages paid to employees						✓

Just checking

Indicate whether each of these statements is true or false.

1 Every transaction is recorded in a book of prime entry. T
2 All cash and credit sales are recorded in the sales daybook. F
3 Books of prime entry are completed at the end of each week. F

Recording transactions relating to credit sales and credit purchases

The documents used in the process of buying and selling goods on credit are featured on pages 68–71. The details from these documents should be recorded in the appropriate book of prime entry.

- When goods are sold to a customer on credit an invoice is sent; the details of the invoice should be recorded in the sales daybook.

- When goods are purchased on credit an invoice will be received from the supplier; the details of the purchase invoice should be recorded in the purchases daybook.

- When goods are returned from a customer a credit note is sent; this is recorded in the sales returns daybook.

- When goods are returned to suppliers a credit note should be received; this is recorded in the purchases returns daybook.

When at work, one of your daily jobs might be to open the post and make a record of all the documents received by post in the appropriate daybook.

Case study

A day in the life of Chanice

Chanice is an accounts assistant at Funky Fashions. She is free to organise her work on a daily basis, but she has set tasks that must be completed each day. She has decided that a fixed routine will help her be more efficient.

She receives a number of financial documents from suppliers, customers and her colleagues. She sorts these documents into the following piles:
- credit notes received from suppliers
- credit notes to be sent to customers
- invoices received from suppliers
- sales invoices to be sent to customers
- remittance advices received from customers.

She puts the remittance advices to one side as she will deal with these later.

First, she works through the sales invoices, recording the details in the sales daybook.

Next, she works through the credit notes received from suppliers, recording the details in the purchases returns daybook.

After this, her next job is to sort through the credit notes to be sent to customers. She records the details of all credit notes in the sales returns daybook.

Finally, she deals with the invoices received. She records each of these in the purchases daybook.

1 What are the four daybooks that Chanice uses each morning as part of her daily routine?

2 In which daybook does she record each of the following documents?

    a Invoice sent to a customer

    b Invoice received from a supplier

    c Credit note sent to a customer

3 When goods are returned to Funky Fashions, a document is sent to the customer showing the amount to be refunded. In which book of prime entry will Chanice enter this document?

    a Cash payments book

    b Purchases returns daybook

    c Sales returns daybook

    d Sales daybook

Activity: Choosing the right book of prime entry

It is important that documents are recorded in the correct book of prime entry, as it is these books that will be used to complete later stages in the accounts process. Match each of the following documents to the appropriate book of prime entry.

Credit note to customer	Sales daybook
Invoice from supplier	Purchases returns daybook
Invoice to customer	Purchases daybook
Credit note received from supplier	Sales returns daybook

Just checking

1 In which book of prime entry should you record a credit sale?

2 In which book of prime entry should you record a credit purchase?

3 In which book of prime entry should you record goods returned from customers?

4 In which book of prime entry should you record goods returned to suppliers?

Recording payments made and monies received

On a day-to-day basis, money will flow in and out of an organisation. This will take various forms, including cash and cheques. You will want to keep an accurate record of all money coming into the organisation from sales and all money going out for goods purchased and in expenses. All **monies** paid and received must be recorded in the correct cash book.

When monies are paid out by the organisation, this should be recorded in the cash payments book. You may record the details of all these payments directly into the cash payments book. Alternatively, you may record the details, the name, payee and amount, in either a **cheques paid listing** or **cash paid listing**. Each day the listings can then be added up and only the daily total entered in the cash payments book. An organisation may make payments using cash, cheques or by transferring money directly from its bank account to the recipient's bank account.

When monies are received by the organisation, this should be recorded in the cash receipts book. Again you may record the details of all receipts directly into the cash receipts book. Alternatively, you may record the details in either the **cheques received listing** or **the cash received listing** and then transfer the daily total to the cash receipts book. Monies received may take the form of cash, cheques or money paid directly into the organisation's bank account. Cash and cheques are paid into the organisation's bank account using a paying-in slip. You will learn more about this on pages 84–85.

Case study

A day in the life of Chanice

Chanice sorts the payments received by Funky Fashions into two piles: one for cash receipts and another for cheques received. She then records the details of all cash receipts in the cash received listing. She writes down the date received, the name of the business or person making the payment and the amount paid. Once she has recorded all of the receipts she adds up the amount column and transfers the total amount to the cash receipts book.

Next she records the details of all the cheques received in the cheques received listing before adding up all the amounts to work out the total value of cheques received for the day. The total amount is then recorded in the cash receipts book.

Later in the day Chanice is given details of all the cash and cheque payments made by Funky Fashions in the day. She records the details of these in the cash paid listing and cheques paid listing before transferring the total amounts to the cash payments book.

For each of the questions below, decide in which of the following Chanice will record the information.

a Cash paid listing
b Cheques paid listing
c Cash received listing
d Cheques received listing
e Cash receipts book
f Cash payments book

1 Where will Chanice record the details of a cheque received from a customer?
2 Where will Chanice record the details of a cheque paid to a supplier?
3 Where will Chanice record the details of cash received from a customer?
4 Where will Chanice record the details of cash paid to a supplier?
5 Where will Chanice record the total value of cheques received from customers?
6 Where will Chanice record the total value of cheques paid to suppliers?

Activity: Which book?

It is important that you enter all documents into the correct book of prime entry. In this activity you will be taking the role of Chanice at Funky Fashions. You will need to use your knowledge from sections 3.2 and 3.3 to identify the relevant book of prime entry for each of the documents shown below.

1

RETRO BAGS
62 West Parade, Selcroft, SE3 6HH

VAT No: 602 123 4567

Invoice No. 2719

To: Funky Fashions   Date: 20 February 20XX
   10 Premier Road, Selcroft, SE2 3TF

Ref: PO Number 361

Item	£
20 bags (purple) @ £15.00	300.00
10 bags (small) @ £6.00	60.00
Sub total	360.00
VAT @ 20%	72.00
Total	**432.00**

Terms: 30 days net

Book of prime entry

Purchase Day Book

2

RETRO BAGS
62 West Parade, Selcroft, SE3 6HH

VAT No: 602 123 4567

Credit note No. 6

To: Funky Fashions   Date: 22 February 20XX
   10 Premier Road, Selcroft, SE2 3TF

Item	£
5 bags (small) @ £6.00	30.00
VAT @ 20%	6.00
Total	**36.00**

Book of prime entry

Purchase returns credit note

3

DB Bank   16-12-79
                        DATE **22 Feb 20XX**

Pay *Funky Fashions*

Seventy pounds only   £ 70.00

Signature *AN Customer*

".018373" 05:63594: 149573"

Book of prime entry

Cash Receipts

Just checking

1   In which book of prime entry will you record payments made?

2   In which book of prime entry will you record monies received?

HW

79

4.1 Types of codes used when recording financial transactions

In a busy accounts office you will be dealing with a large number of transactions from many customers and suppliers.

Codes are often used to make it easier to cross-reference the documents to suppliers and customers. Each supplier and customer will be given a unique code. You will then be able to retrieve information about the customer or supplier quickly by using this unique code. This system also makes it easier to group information. For example, you might want to make a list of all the orders made by a particular customer.

When at work you might use one of three methods of coding. These methods are **alphabetical**, **numerical** and **alphanumerical**. Alphabetical codes only use letters, numerical codes only use numbers, and alphanumerical codes use a combination of letters and numbers.

Worked example

Codes in practice

Style Superstores allocates alphabetical codes to all its suppliers as shown below:

Supplier	Department	Unique code
Jack's Fisheries, Whitby	Fresh fish	FFJW
Filey Fishmongers, Filey	Fresh fish	FFFF
Ridge Farm, Wetherby	Meat and poultry	MPRW

Trotter Traders allocates numerical codes to all its customers as shown below:

Customer	Department	Unique code
Jack's Fisheries, Whitby	Fresh fish	10001
Filey Fishmongers, Filey	Fresh fish	10002
Ridge Farm, Wetherby	Meat and poultry	20001

Regency Minimarkets allocates alphanumerical codes to all its suppliers as shown below:

Supplier	Department	Unique code
Jack's Fisheries, Whitby	Fresh fish	FF0001
Filey Fishmongers, Filey	Fresh fish	FF0002
Ridge Farm, Wetherby	Meat and poultry	MP0001

1 Which organisation might use the code 60009?

2 Which organisation might use the code CC0008?

3 Which organisation only uses letters in its codes?

Activity: Credit or cash?

Office Furniture Ltd uses all three types of coding systems. It gives all suppliers a numerical code, but customers can be given either an alphabetical or an alphanumerical code.

Customers are allocated a code based on the first three letters of their organisation name. Some customers are expected to pay immediately and their code is alphabetical. Other customers are given either 30 or 60 days to pay, and the appropriate number is added to their code.

Smith Secretarial College, for example, has a 30-day credit term agreed with Office Furniture Ltd, and its code is therefore SMI30.

Identify with a tick ✔ in the right box, whether each of these codes belongs to a supplier, cash customer or credit customer.

Code	Supplier	Cash customer	Credit customer
MON30			✓
BRO		✓	
00098	✓		
SIN60			✓
FRO30			✓
TRE		✓	
00165	✓		

Just checking

Indicate whether each of these statements is true or false.

1 In a numerical coding system, all codes consist of numbers and letters.

2 In an alphabetical coding system, all codes consist of letters only.

3 BRO55 is an example of an alphanumerical code.

HW

Transactions take place in most organisations on a regular basis throughout the day. These can be dealt with one at a time as they occur or stored up to process all together. If documents such as invoices and credit notes are stored up and then processed together, this is called **batch processing**. This means that all the invoices will be processed as a batch.

In a busy workplace, batch processing will help to save time. It means that employees can focus on one task at a time rather than swapping between tasks and books of prime entry.

Case study

Danny's day

Danny works at a firm of solicitors. He is responsible for making sure that all daily financial transactions are recorded in the correct book of prime entry. Each day he uses six different daybooks:

- sales daybook
- sales returns daybook
- cash receipts book
- purchases daybook
- purchases returns daybook
- cash payments book.

At the end of each day the solicitors pass their timesheets to the accounts department and Danny's colleague uses these to produce sales invoices. The first thing Danny does each day is work through the previous day's sales invoices. He writes the information in the sales daybook before sending the invoices to the clients.

By the time Danny has finished doing this, the post has normally arrived. Danny opens all the post and splits it into piles:

- invoices received from suppliers
- credit notes received from suppliers
- remittance advices received from customers.

Victoria used to do this job before Danny, and she would deal with each item as she opened it. She thought this saved handling documents twice. However, Danny thought this was inefficient and preferred to sort the documents first, then deal with them in batches. He thought this was quicker because, although he had to put them into piles, he could put all the entries into one daybook at a time.

1 In which book of prime entry will Danny enter the following?
   a Purchase invoices
   b Purchase credit notes
   c Cash received listings

2 Does Danny use a batch processing system?

3 Did Victoria use a batch processing system?

Activity: Advantages and disadvantages of batch control systems

When at work you may be responsible for deciding how to organise your workload in the best way. You saw that Danny and Victoria took different approaches.

Think about the advantages and disadvantages of batch processing rather than handling each transaction as it arises.

Do you think you will use batch processing or individual transaction processing at work?

Just checking

Indicate whether each of these statements is true or false.

1 Batch processing involves dealing with all similar transactions in one go.

2 Batch processing is slower than individual transaction processing.

3 In batch processing, when a customer makes a payment it will be entered into the cash receipts book immediately.

The income of an organisation comes from making sales. Many customers choose to pay in cash or by writing a **cheque**. Although the organisation may keep some of the cash to meet day-to-day expenditure, it will want to pay most of the money into the bank.

If you are asked at work to pay money into the bank, you will need to complete a bank **paying-in slip**. This document tells the bank how much money is being paid in as notes, coins and cheques.

Someone within the finance department will usually be responsible for counting the money to be paid in and for filling in the paying-in slip. It may also be their job to take the money to the bank.

Worked example

Paying in money to the bank

The bank will provide an organisation with a book of paying-in slips. One slip needs to be filled in every time money is taken to the bank. It is important that you fill in the slip accurately. It is also important to complete the stub that stays in the book, as this acts as a record for the organisation. In order to complete a paying-in slip, you should take the following steps.

1 Paying in cash (notes and coins)

- Bring all the cash that you are going to pay in together, and group the notes and coins in order of value. So, all the £20 notes will be grouped together, all the £1 coins will be grouped together, and so on.
- Count how much money you have for each type of note and coin. For example, if you have two £50 notes, then write down £100. (If you are paying in a lot of cash, an organisation will use the cash bags that are available from the bank.)
- Write all this down on a piece of paper and check it by repeating the process, and ticking if the figure is correct. You will need to record how much you have in £2, £1 and 50p coins, and other silver and bronze.
- You can now transfer this information to the paying-in slip (see Figure 3.4).

2 Total cash

- You should now have filled in the grid on the right of the paying-in slip with details of all the notes and coins.
- Add these together to work out the total amount of cash, and write this on the slip and the stub. It is worth adding it up twice to check that you are correct.

3 Paying in cheques

- On the back of the paying-in slip, write a list of the cheques. For each cheque you need to write down the name of the customer and the amount.
- Add up the value of the cheques and write the total at the bottom of the back of the slip.
- Transfer this total to the front of the slip and the stub.
- Count how many cheques you have and write this in the box on the front of the slip where it says "no. of cheques" (see Figure 3.4).

4 Calculating the total
- Add the total cash and total cheques together.
- Record this on the paying-in slip and the stub.

5 Completing the paying-in slip
- Write the date on both the stub and paying-in slip.
- Write the name of the person who will be paying the money in.

stub

Date: 1/11/2014	Date: 1/11/2014	**City Bank plc Redport**	£50 notes	
A/C 10678465 J.Gardener Limited.			£20 notes	80.00
			£10 notes	100.00
Cash: 315.00		Account J.Gardener Limited.	£5 notes	80.00
			£2 coin	
Cheques, POs: 1000.00	No. of cheques 1		£1 coin	50.00
		Paid in by MOHAMED ISMAIL	Other coin	5.00
Total: 1315.00			Total cash	315.00
			Cheques, POs	1000.00
000001		30-45-22 10678465	Total £	1315.00

Figure 3.4: A bank paying-in slip

Activity: Paying-in slips

You are now going to practise completing a bank paying-in slip for J. Gardener Limited.

You have been asked to pay some money into the bank. Use the information provided below to complete the paying-in slip for J. Gardener Limited.

Notes:
4 × £20 notes
10 × £10 notes
16 × £5 notes

Cash:
50 × £1 coins
£5 in 20p coins

Cheques:
Glenn £1,000.00

Just checking

1 What is a paying-in slip?
2 Why is it important to complete paying-in slips accurately?
3 What techniques can you use to check that a paying-in slip is completed accurately?

An organisation might choose to pay for items by cheque. This is often an easier and safer method of payment than cash, particularly if large sums of money are involved or the payment is being sent in the post. When making a payment by cheque, the money is transferred from one bank account to another.

When an organisation receives invoices, these will be passed to the finance department. The cashier is responsible for making and recording payments in the cash payments book. The cashier will be authorised to write a business cheque, although it may need two signatures to be valid.

Worked example

How to write a cheque

When writing a cheque it is important to complete both the cheque and the stub carefully. If a cheque is completed incorrectly, then it will be returned to the organisation, and this may delay receipt of an order. Figure 3.5 shows how a cheque must be filled in.

Stub: Transfer all the information on to the stub. This acts as your record.

Pay: On the first line, write the name of the **payee** (the person or organisation that the cheque is being sent to).

Date: This is the date that the cheque is written.

In the box write the amount in numbers. This must be the same as the written amount.

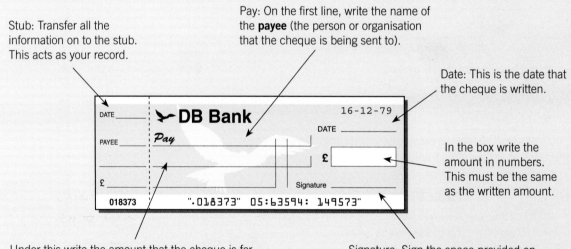

Under this write the amount that the cheque is for. The pounds part of this must be written in words, but the pence can be written in numbers. If the amount is a whole number of pounds – that is, the sum has no pence – then you should write "only" after you have written the amount of pounds in words. For example to write a cheque for £150.00, write "One hundred and fifty pounds only".

Signature: Sign the space provided on the bottom right of the cheque if you are authorised to do so. Your organisation may have a policy of having more than one **signatory**, *if so both people must sign here.*

Figure 3.5: How to complete a cheque

Activity: Writing a cheque

You have been asked to write out a cheque to pay an invoice received by your organisation. Use the information provided in the invoice below to complete a blank cheque. Remember that it is unlikely that you will receive the invoice on the same day that it is sent, so you should fill in the date on the cheque as 20 November 20XX.

ABC Electronic Supplies

23 Main Street, Washington, NE2 6QP
Tel: 0191 458921

INVOICE

Date: 17 November 20XX

Invoice No: 2378

Bill address:
Sparks Ltd
Unit 4, Valley Trading Estate
Leeds LS3 7TW

Delivery address:
Same as billing address

P.O. No.	Sales Rep Name	Delivery date	Delivery via	Due Date
020061 2005	Sales 1	17/11/200XX	Courier	

Product ID	Description	Quantity	Unit Price	Line Total
P1003	Handset	10	420.00	4,200.00
P1000	Bluetooth headset	12	199.99	2,399.88
P1004	Non-taxable item	5	200.00	1,000.00
P1002	Serviceplan	4	204.41	817.64
P1006	Smartphone	10	500.00	5,000.00

Notes:	Sub total	13,417.52
	VAT	2,683.50
	Shipping & handling	–
	Total	16,101.02
	Paid	–
	Total due	16,101.02

DATE 20 Nov 20XX
DB Bank 16-12-79
PAYEE ABC Electro DATE 20-Nov
Pay ABC Electronic
Electro SixTEEN Thousand £ 16,101.02
£16,101.02 One HUNDRED and One Pound And 2 pence
and 2p Signature A McJ...

018373 "018373" 05:63594: 149573"

Just checking

1 What is a cheque?

2 When might an organisation prefer to make payments by cheque?

3 Why is it important to complete the stub as well as the cheque?

Key terms

Gross profit: The amount of money left from sales after the cost of sales has been deducted.

Cost of sales: The direct cost of producing the goods and services that have been sold. For example, raw materials for a manufacturing organisation, or products to sell for a retailing organisation. Organisations that provide services often have a very small cost of sales.

At the end of each year, or possibly twice a year, organisations will produce a statement of profit. This summarises the income and expenditure of the organisation over the preceding time period.

The statement of profit shows two different profit figures. The first one is **gross profit**. This is calculated as sales minus **cost of sales**.

This is not, however, the final profit figure, because it doesn't take into account all the other expenses of the organisation. The second one is net profit. You will learn more about this on pages 90–91.

As you know, your work in an accounting office will involve recording transactions on a daily basis. At set points in time, the organisation will want to know how it has performed overall, and this is when the information in its financial records is used to calculate a gross profit figure.

Worked example

The market stall

You have offered to help some friends calculate their gross profit at the end of their first year of selling knitwear on a market stall. They have recorded that the total sales made over the year was £60,000, and it cost them £45,000 to buy the knitwear.

Sales = £60,000   Cost of sales = £45,000   Gross profit = £15,000

Sales – cost of sales = gross profit

Laura Jack, MAAT

The gross profit of an MP3 player would be the income from selling the device minus the cost of the raw materials and manufacturing.

Activity: Calculating gross profit

Use the information shown below to calculate the gross profit for Emmanuel's Events Ltd.

    Sales are £2,500 per month

    Cost of sales is 40% of sales

1 Calculate Emmanuel's annual sales. *30,000*

2 Calculate Emmanuel's annual cost of sales. *12,000*

3 Subtract Emmanuel's cost of sales from his annual sales to work out his gross profit for the year. *18,000*

Mathematics for accounting

Last year your organisation recorded sales of £76,000 and achieved a gross profit of £12,000. Calculate the cost of sales.

Just checking ☑

1 What is the gross profit for an organisation with sales of £49,000 and cost of sales of £19,600? *£29400*

2 What is the gross profit as a percentage of sales for the organisation in question 1?

3 After deducting cost of sales of £38,000, an organisation has a gross profit of £3,500. What was its sales?

4 An organisation has achieved a 20% gross profit on sales of £100,000. What is the gross profit figure?

6.2 Net profit or loss

Key term

Net profit: The amount left from sales income after cost of sales and all other expenses have been deducted.

On pages 88–89 you saw how to calculate gross profit. You are now going to take this a step further to calculate **net profit**. This is the profit left after all the other expenses have been deducted.

Gross profit = Sales – cost of sales

Net profit = Gross profit – expenses

When working in a finance office, you will be interested in the gross profit. But your boss may be more interested in the net profit, as this is the true measure of how an organisation is performing.

Worked example

The market stall

You have offered to help friends calculate their gross and net profit at the end of their first year of selling knitwear on a market stall. They have recorded that their total sales over the year was £60,000 and that to buy the knitwear cost them £45,000.

Sales – cost of sales = gross profit

However this is not the final figure. Your friends have also had to pay £500 a month to rent the market stall. In addition, they have incurred other expenses equal to £3,000.

First, we need to calculate their total expenses. These are:

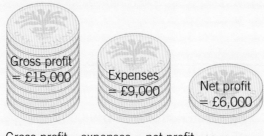

Gross profit – expenses = net profit

Activity: Net profit

This table shows the sales, cost of sales and expenses for your organisation over the first three years of trading.

1 Use the information to calculate the gross profit and net profit or loss for each year.

2 Once you have completed this, calculate the net profit as a percentage of sales for each year in the final row of the table.

	Year 1	Year 2	Year 3
Sales	£32,000	£56,000	£70,000
Cost of sales	£20,000	£29,000	£35,000
Gross profit	£12,000	£27,000	£35,000
Expenses	£17,000	£27,000	£27,000
Net profit/loss	-5000	—	8000
Net profit as a percentage of sales			

Mathematics for accounting

Last year your organisation recorded income and expenditure as shown below.

Income and expenditure	£
Sales	150,000
Cost of sales	74,000
Wages	20,000
Marketing	3,000
Postage	800
Utilities	1,500

Use this information to calculate:

a gross profit

b total expenses

c net profit.

Just checking

1 An organisation has gross profit of £48,000 and expenses of £50,000. What is the net profit or loss?

2 An organisation has sales of £20,000, cost of sales of £12,000 and expenses of £5,000. What is the net profit or loss?

3 Using your answer to question 2, what is the net profit as a percentage of sales?

4 An organisation has expenses of £1,200, £1,500, £12,000 and £800. Its gross profit is £20,000. What is its net profit?

Check your understanding

Before you start this test of your knowledge and understanding, review the statements in the "Before you start" feature on page 57 and decide how confident you feel about the topics covered in this unit.

1   Select which **one** of the following statements describes an asset.

   a   An asset is something an organisation receives from customers.

   b   An asset is something an organisation owes.

   c   An asset is something an organisation owns.

2   What is money received from sales called?

   a   An asset

   b   Income

   c   Expenditure

3   Use the appropriate word from the list below to identify each key term being described.
   Words: asset, liability, creditor, debtor, cash sale, credit sale, cash purchase, credit purchase

   a   Someone an organisation owes money to for goods purchased on credit   *Creditor*

   b   A transaction to sell goods when payment is delayed   *debtor / credit sale*

   c   A transaction to purchase goods when payment is immediate   *cash purchase*

   d   Money owed by an organisation

4   If a supplier allows its customers 30 days to pay, what is this an example of?

   a   a cash transaction

   b   a credit transaction

5   Use a tick ✔ to identify which document would be used in each of the following transactions.

Transaction	Purchase order	Credit note	Invoice	Remittance advice
A customer returns faulty goods				✔
A customer uses a bank transfer to pay an invoice		✔	✔	
A supplier requests payment			✔	

6   Which book of prime entry would the following documents be entered into?

   a   Credit note sent to a customer

   b   Credit note received from a supplier

   c   Cheque received from a customer

7 Select which one of these documents would be entered in the purchases daybook.

   a A credit note sent to a customer

   b A cheque sent to a supplier

   c A purchase invoice sent to a supplier

8 Show whether the following statement is true or false.
In an alphanumerical coding system, all codes consist of letters only.

   a True   b False

9 Show whether the following statement is true or false.
In a batch processing system, all cheques received in one day are entered into the cash receipts book at the same time.

   a True   b False

10 Complete the paying-in slip.

   a Two £50 notes

   b Six £5 notes

   c Ten £1 coins

   d Four 50p coins

   e One cheque for £525.50

Date:	Date:	City Bank plc Redport	£50 notes	
A/C			£20 notes	
			£10 notes	
Cash:		Account	£5 notes	
			£2 coin	
Cheques, POs:	No. of cheques		£1 coin	
		Paid in by	Other coin	
Total:			Total cash	
			Cheques, POs	
000001		30-45-22 10678465	Total £	

11 Show whether the following statement is true or false.
A paying-in slip should list details of all cheques on the back.

   a True   b False

12 Show whether the following statement is true or false.
A cheque should be signed by the payee.

   a True   b False

13 Complete the following sentence by selecting the most appropriate word from the list below:

same as, higher than, lower than

When income is _____ expenses an organisation has made a loss.

14 Look at the following table of income and expenditure and answer the questions below.

Income and expenditure	£
Sales	250,000
Cost of sales	130,000
Wages	65,500
Office expenses	25,000
Selling expenses	13,000

   a Calculate gross profit.

   b Calculate net profit.

   c What is net profit as a percentage of sales?

Unit 4:
Mathematics for accounting

Introduction

In your work in the finance department of an organisation you will be handling money and working with numbers on a daily basis. It is essential that you are able to use basic mathematical concepts accurately and with confidence.

You will be able to use a standard calculator, so you won't need to carry out these tasks in your head. However, it is important to know and understand how to perform specific calculations in order to get accurate results.

By the end of this unit you will be able to:

- add and subtract whole numbers, and numbers up to two decimal places
- multiply and divide whole numbers, and numbers up to two decimal places
- calculate the ratio or proportion of two numbers
- calculate the percentage of one number in relation to another number
- find a percentage of a whole number
- apply fractions to whole numbers
- calculate the average of a range of numbers.

Claire Weingaertner, Member in practice of Focus Accounting

Mathematics doesn't have to be difficult, it is just a matter of taking one step at a time.

Before you start

Read the statements below and decide how much you agree with them.

	Agree	Not sure	Disagree
I am able to add whole numbers and numbers up to two decimal places.			
I am able to subtract whole numbers and numbers up to two decimal places.			
I am able to multiply whole numbers and numbers up to two decimal places.			
I am able to divide whole numbers and numbers up to two decimal places.			
I can calculate the ratio or proportion of two numbers.			
I can calculate the percentage of one number in relation to another number.			
I can find the percentage of a whole number.			
I am able to apply fractions to whole numbers.			
I am able to calculate the average of a range of numbers.			

1.1

Add and subtract whole numbers, and numbers up to two decimal places

Key term

Decimals: A fraction of a number that is written using the decimal system. This is indicated by the use of the decimal point (.).

At work there will be a wide range of tasks that require you to add and subtract numbers. For example, a customer may have ordered five different items and you will need to be able to calculate the total cost to produce a sales invoice. When calculating whether a business has made a profit or a loss, you will need to be able to subtract expenses from income.

It is important to remember that most of the time when working with numbers in a finance department, you will be dealing with figures that represent sums of money. Therefore, it is necessary to deal with whole numbers, such as £1,000, as well as **decimals** such as £1.2 million and £19.99.

Worked example

Add and subtract

You will need to add and subtract numbers to calculate an organisation's net profit (see pages 66–67).

1 An organisation has the following expenses. You will need to add these expenses to calculate the total expenses.

Wages	£60,000.00	+
Marketing	£1,700.00	+
Administration	£999.50	+
Travel	£3,000.00	+
Heat and light	£2,500.99	
Total expenses	**£68,200.49**	

2 The organisation has sales of £350,000.00. The cost of these sales was £170,000.00. In order to calculate the gross profit, you need to subtract the cost of sales from the sales.

Sales	£350,000.00	–
Cost of sales	£170,000.00	
Gross profit	**£180,000.00**	

3 Finally, to calculate the net profit, you will need to subtract the expenses (calculated in step 1) from the gross profit (calculated in step 2).

Gross profit	£180,000.00	–
Total expenses	£68,200.49	
Net profit	**£111,799.51**	

Activity: Add and subtract

When sending out an invoice to a customer, it is important that it is accurate. If it contains an error, it might mean the customer is being charged too little (which won't make your employer happy) or is being charged too much (which won't make the customer happy).

Complete this invoice to calculate the total amount owed by the customer.

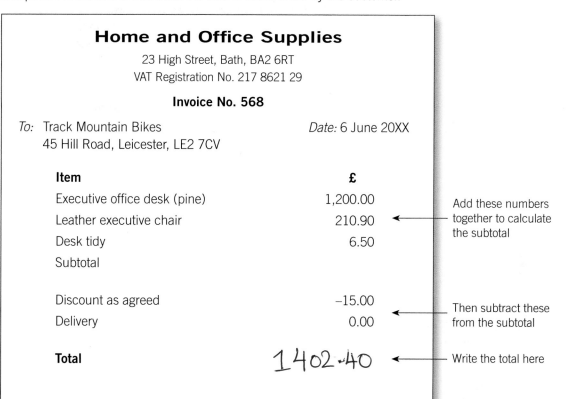

Home and Office Supplies

23 High Street, Bath, BA2 6RT

VAT Registration No. 217 8621 29

Invoice No. 568

To: Track Mountain Bikes   Date: 6 June 20XX
     45 Hill Road, Leicester, LE2 7CV

Item	£
Executive office desk (pine)	1,200.00
Leather executive chair	210.90	← Add these numbers together to calculate the subtotal
Desk tidy	6.50
Subtotal	
Discount as agreed	−15.00
Delivery	0.00	← Then subtract these from the subtotal
Total	*1402·40*	← Write the total here

Terms: 30 days net

Just checking

1 Sweet Success has sales of £125,789.25 and cost of sales of £78,007.89. What is the gross profit? (Check the worked example if you are unsure.)

2 Sweet Success has expenses as follows:
   • Wages £45,000.00
   • Marketing £2,899.00
   • Heat and light £1,500.75
   • Administration £2,000.00
   • Other £1,950.99
   What are its total expenses?

3 An organisation has sales of £2.9 million and cost of sales of £1.3 million. What is the organisation's gross profit?

4 Suppose you have received an invoice for an order totalling £3,500.00, but you have returned three of the items listed on the invoice. The returned items cost £600.00, £25.99 and £100.05. What is the new total amount owing?

1.2 Multiply and divide whole numbers, and numbers up to two decimal places

When working in your finance office, there will be occasions when you will need to multiply and divide numbers. For example, you may want to buy more than one of an item, so when completing the purchase order you will need to multiply the unit price by the quantity required to get the total price.

You may find that you need to use division to split expenditure equally between more than one department. For example, if an organisation spends £2,500 on a summer party for its staff, it may decide to split the cost of the party equally between its departments. If there are five separate departments in the organisation it means that each department needs to contribute £500 (£2,500 divided by 5).

Worked example

Multiply and divide

A bicycle shop is placing an order with one of its suppliers for some new bike accessories. The manager has asked you to calculate the total cost of the order.

The manager has asked for:

- 10 disc brakes @ £60.00 each
- 12 front and rear lights @ £18.00 per set
- 5 child seats @ £68.99
- 1 heart-rate monitor @ £299.50

The best way to do this is to set out the information in a table with four columns like the one below.

Item	Quantity	Unit price	Total price

1 In the table, place all the items in column 1, the quantity required in column 2 and the unit price in column 3.

2 Then multiply the quantity (column 2) figure by the unit price (column 3) to find the total price (column 4) for each item. Write this in column 4.

3 You can then add the figures in column 4 to get the total cost of the order.

Item	Quantity	Unit price	Total price
Disc brakes	10	£60.00	£600.00
Front and rear lights	12	£18.00	£216.00
Child seats	5	£68.99	£344.95
Heart-rate monitor	1	£299.50	£299.50
Total			£1,460.45

The manager is also considering importing some inner tubes. He can purchase a box of 500 for £780. He has asked you to calculate the unit cost of these inner tubes.

We know that: $\text{Unit cost} = \dfrac{\text{Total cost}}{\text{Number of units}}$

So, in this case: $\text{Unit cost} = \dfrac{\text{Total cost}}{\text{Number of units}} = \dfrac{£780}{500} = £1.56$

Myra Geater, MAAT

Accountants need to use simple mathematics, such as multiplication and division, on a daily basis – even for some of the more advanced accounting tasks.

Activity: Multiply and divide

You are going to practise multiplying and dividing by calculating the cost to a local business of hosting a training event in a hotel in Birmingham. Use the information provided below to calculate the total cost of hosting a training day in Birmingham for 25 delegates.

Birmingham training day costs

Item	Price
Room hire	£250.00
Welcome refreshments	£2.60 per delegate
Lunch	£25.50 per delegate
Refreshments	£3.00 per delegate
Hire of laptop and projector	£150.00

Once you have calculated the total cost, work out what the cost per delegate would be.

Just checking

1 Maxwell sells 320 sweatshirts at £19.99 each. What are his total sales?

2 Sharma buys 1,500 bottles of mineral water for £870. What is the cost of one bottle of water?

3 Monkey Madness, a children's indoor play centre, has a busy Saturday as it is visited by 42 children accompanied by 15 adults. The entry price for each child is £5.99, and the price for adults is £10.00. What is the total sales for the day?

251.58
150.00
40 ✓ 58 HW

1.3

Calculate the ratio or proportion of two numbers

Key term

Ratio: The amount of one number in relation to another number. The numbers are always separated by a colon (:).

A **ratio** is when the amount of one number is expressed in relation to another number. Ratios are written as:

One number : The other number

For example, on a bus there may be one driver to 40 passengers. This is a ratio of 1:40. If neither of the numbers in your ratio is 1, you need to divide one number by another. Say there were two drivers on the bus, but still 40 passengers. Dividing 40 passengers by 2 bus drivers will give you 20. This means that the ratio of bus drivers to passengers is 1:20.

In a finance office you might analyse income or purchases by using ratios. You might want to know what proportion of total sales comes from a particular product line, or what proportion of total expenses is the result of one type of expenditure, such as wages.

For example, if you want to know what costs are as a proportion of sales, you divide the costs by the sales. Then you would write the result as follows, putting your answer rather than the formula in the second part of the expression:

$$1 : \frac{\text{costs}}{\text{sales}}$$

Worked example

Ratios and proportions

These are two examples of situations when you could be asked to calculate a ratio in business. The main purpose is to make it easier to analyse figures.

Example 1

An organisation has total expenses of £150,000 of which £50,000 is wages. The manager wants to know what the ratio is of expenses to wages.

To do this, divide expenses by wages:

$$\frac{£150,000}{£50,000} = 3$$

Then express the answer as a ratio: 3:1.

This means that for every £3 the organisation spends on expenses, £1 will be spent on wages.

Example 2

An organisation sells its goods in the UK and in the USA. It wants to know what the ratio of UK sales is to USA sales. Each year it has sales of £100,000 to its UK customers and £500,000 to its USA customers.

Divide USA sales by UK sales.

$$\frac{£500,000}{£100,000} = 5$$

The ratio is therefore 1:5. This means that for every £1 worth of sales in the UK, it can expect to have sales of £5 in the USA.

Activity: Ratios and proportions

WM Manufacturing employs 100 people. Use ratios to answer the following questions.

1 Of WM Manufacturing's employees, 25 are part-time and 75 are full-time employees. What is the ratio of part-time employees to full-time employees? *1:3*

2 Of WM Manufacturing's employees, 20 earn £25,000 or more and 80 earn £24,999 or less. What is the ratio of employees earning £25,000 or more to those earning less? *1:4*

3 WM Manufacturing spends £2,500,000 on wages and £5,000,000 on machinery. What is the ratio of money spent on machinery to wages? *2:1*

Just checking

You will need to consult this income and expenses table to answer the questions that follow.

Income and expenses	£
Sales	225,000
Cost of sales	75,000
Wages	25,000
Marketing	12,500
Administration	9,250
Other	3,250

1 What is the ratio of cost of sales to sales? *1:3*

2 Calculate the ratio of the total expenses (wages + marketing + administration + other) to the wages. *2:1*

3 What is the ratio of marketing spend to sales? *1:18*

1.4

Calculate the percentage of one number in relation to another number

A percentage is a way of expressing a number out of 100. It makes it much easier to compare figures. If, for example, a student gets 25 in test 1 and 80 in test 2, we can't assume that the student did better in the second test, as we don't know how many marks were available in each test. For example, the student might have got 25 out of 25 in test 1, scoring 100%, but only 80 out of 100 in test 2, scoring 80%.

To calculate a percentage, you divide one number by the other and multiply the answer by 100. To work out 20 as a percentage of 80, you do the following calculation:

$$\frac{20}{80} \times 100 = 25\%$$

Sometimes organisations will use percentages in a similar way to ratios. For example, they may want to know what percentage of their expenditure is spent on wages.

Worked example

Cottingham Coaches

Terry Cottingham, the Managing Director of Cottingham Coaches, is reviewing his organisation's spending. He wants to know what percentage of his total expenditure goes on his coaches.

Expenses	Value
Wages	£33,000
Office rent	£12,000
Coach maintenance	£9,500
Coach insurance	£6,500
Fuel	£14,000

1 As a first step, you need to calculate the total expenses by adding all the individual expenses together. This gives you a total of £75,000.

2 Next, you need to calculate the total expenditure linked to the coaches by adding coach maintenance, coach insurance and fuel. This gives you a total of £30,000.

3 To calculate the percentage:

   a Divide £30,000 by £75,000. This will give you 0.4.

   b Multiple 0.4 by 100. This will give you the answer: 40%.

   This means that 40% of Cottingham Coaches' expenditure goes on the coaches.

Activity: Council tax bands

Council tax is calculated on the value of a property and charged each year. You work for a local council and your manager wants to work out what percentage of properties within the area are covered by which council tax band.

1 Use the information in the table below to calculate the percentage of the total number of properties in the area that fall into each council tax band.

Council tax band	No. of properties	% of total
A	3,055	3.25
B	15,980	17.00
C	50,760	54.00
D	20,210	21.50
E	3,995	4.25
Total no. of properties	**94,000**	100

2 Check your workings by adding the percentages in the third column together. If they come to 100%, your answers are likely to be correct.

Just checking

1 A business has sales of £276,000 and gross profit of £66,240. What is gross profit as a percentage of sales?   24%

2 A business has sales of £276,000 and net profit of £12,420. What is net profit as a percentage of sales?   4.5%

3 A business has total expenses of £125,000 and wages of £35,550. What percentage of total expenses is wages?   28.44

1.5 Find a percentage of a whole number

At work there may be occasions when you need to calculate a percentage of a whole number.

You may also find that a customer has been offered a percentage discount. You need to be able to calculate the discount in order to deduct it from the customer's invoice.

To calculate the percentage of a whole number, you take two steps:

1 Divide the number by 100 (this calculates what 1% of the number is).

2 Multiply this by the percentage you want to find. For example, for VAT this would be 20% (at 2012 tax rates).

Worked example

Cost of a conference room

Jane Smith is a professional trainer and has booked a conference room at a London hotel to host a training event for a customer. There will be 30 delegates, and the hotel charges a daily delegate rate of £90 per delegate. The hotel has agreed to give Jane a 5% discount.

30 delegates at £90 = £2,700

Less 5% discount:

$$\frac{£2,700}{100} = £27$$

$$£27 \times 5 = £135$$
$$£2,700 - £135 = £2,565$$

The total cost of the hotel booking is £2,565.
Jane wants to make a profit on the training event by charging the customer. She decides that she wants to charge the client the cost of the event plus 60%.

$$\frac{£2,565}{100} = £25.65$$

$$£25.65 \times 60 = £1,539$$
$$£1,539 + £2,565 = £4,104$$

The total amount Jane will charge the customer is £4,104.

Activity: Percentages

You are going to practise calculating percentages by completing an invoice that shows both a discount and VAT. To do this, complete the invoice below.

✓

HW

Sparkle Cleaning Supplies

**29 Trent Avenue,
Nottingham, NG24 6LK**

VAT no: 789 1237654

Invoice no. C00098

To: Clarke and Co Solicitors   Date: 30 June 20XX
Reading Square, Office 2B,
Bury, CE4 6NB

Industrial carpet shampoo	£28.00
Super z35 floor polisher	£357.00
Bulk purchase bin liners	£15.00

Total order:
Less 10% discount
Total after discount
VAT at 20%
Total

Terms: 30 days net

Just checking

1 How much VAT (at 20%) would be charged on an order of £2,500? ,500

2 An order for £37,500 receives a 12% discount.
   a What is the value of the discount? £4,500
   b What is the value of the order after discount? 33,000
   c How much VAT (at 20%) would be charged? 6,600
   d What is the final value of the order?

3 A retailer offers a customer a 10% discount on a jumper because it is slightly damaged. The retail price of the jumper is £190. How much would the customer now pay? £171

4 A UK business has total sales of £458,000 of which 28% is from sales overseas. What is the value of UK sales? £128,240

329,760

Apply fractions to whole numbers

Fraction: A way of showing a part of a whole number without presenting it as a decimal.

Denominator: The number on the bottom of the fraction.

Numerator: The number on the top of the fraction.

A **fraction** is a part of a whole number. In a business, you might, for example, find that $\frac{1}{2}$ (a half) of sales comes from a particular product range or that raw materials account for $\frac{1}{3}$ (a third) of all costs.

The number on the bottom of the fraction is called the **denominator**, and the number on top the **numerator**. In the fraction $\frac{3}{10}$, for example, 10 is the denominator and 3 the numerator. Knowing this will help you apply fractions to whole numbers as shown in the worked example.

Sanaz Amidi, MAAT

Fractions are a useful way of presenting information. For example, if a report shows that only $\frac{1}{9}$ of all paintings sold by a gallery are framed, the gallery might decide to try to sell more frames to increase its sales.

Worked example

Fractions

Suppose an attraction had 300 visitors in a day and $\frac{2}{5}$ of these used a discount voucher. We want to calculate how many visitors used a discount voucher.

Do this as follows.

First divide the number of customers by the denominator:

$$\frac{300}{5} = 60$$

Then multiply the answer by the numerator:

$$60 \times 2 = 120$$

So, 120 customers used the discount voucher.

Activity: Fractions

1 Rockingham Restaurant has served 1,200 customers in the last week, of which $\frac{2}{3}$ used a discount voucher. How many customers used the discount voucher? *800 Customers*

2 A business has sales of £340,000. It estimates that $\frac{3}{5}$ of its sales are in the UK. How much are the UK sales worth? *204,000*

3 An organisation has 27 employees, and $\frac{1}{3}$ of these employees work in the Glasgow office. How many employees work in the Glasgow office? *9*

4 An organisation is looking at its expenditure and sales. It estimates that for every £1 it receives in sales, it spends $\frac{1}{4}$ on marketing. How much does the organisation spend on marketing for each £1 it receives in sales? *£0.25*

Just checking

1 What is $\frac{1}{2}$ of 5,000?

2 If a firm has 25,000 customers of whom $\frac{3}{8}$ are children, how many children are customers?

3 Is $\frac{2}{5}$ the same as $\frac{4}{10}$?

4 £300 is $\frac{2}{3}$ of £900. Is this true or false?

Calculate the average of a range of numbers

An **average** is one number that represents the typical value of all items in a list of numbers. For example, a business might want to know how much an average customer spends or what its average weekly sales are.

To calculate an average, you add up all the values in a list and divide by the number of items. If, for example, a business is open Monday to Friday and, during the week, its daily sales are: £240, £200, £199, £321 and £304, then the average daily sales would be £252.80 ($\frac{£1,264}{5}$).

Averages can help an organisation make important decisions. For example, if the average amount a customer spends at a café is £4.36, the owner may decide to try to attract more customers rather than try to get each customer to spend more.

Worked example

Mildred's Café

The owner of Mildred's Café wants to know the average daily sales total for a weekday. The daily sales figures of the business for the past week are as follows:

Monday	Tuesday	Wednesday	Thursday	Friday
£300	£350	£290	£300	£430

In order to calculate the average, you need to take two steps.

First, add all five numbers together.

300 + 350 + 290 + 300 + 430 = £1,670

Second, divide the total by the number of items:

$$\frac{£1,670}{5} = £334$$

The average daily sales is £334.

Jessica D'Aulerio, MAAT

A café can use averages to work out how much a typical customer spends.

Activity: Averages

Suppose you work for a new business that has been trading for just four months. These are the sales figures for each month.

Month	Sales (£)
1	1,325.00
2	1,330.99
3	1,657.79
4	2,150.50

1 What has been the average monthly sales for the first four months?   1616.07

2 In month 5, sales are £1,750.02. Has the average monthly sales gone up or down?

Just checking

1 A car showroom sells three cars in a day. The first car costs £9,000 and the other two cars cost £13,500. What is the average cost of the cars sold?   7500

2 Customer numbers in a coffee shop are:

Monday	25
Tuesday	45
Wednesday	86
Thursday	74
Friday	92

64.4

What is the average number of customers per day?

3 A business employs four sales assistants. Two are paid £5.93 per hour, and the other two are paid £6.25 per hour. What is the average hourly wage?   £6.09

Check your understanding

Before you start this test of your knowledge and understanding, review the statements in the "Before you start" feature on page 95 and decide how confident you feel about the topics covered in this unit.

1   You work for a gardening company.

   a   You have been asked to complete an invoice by your manager. Calculate the total sales value for each item.

   3 fence panels @ £12.50 each
   5 fence posts @ £7.25 each
   1 bag cement @ £5.25 each

   b   What is the subtotal of the order?

   c   The customer has a credit note for £5.00, which needs to be subtracted from the subtotal. What is the subtotal now?

   d   You now need to calculate VAT at 20% and add this to the subtotal to produce the total. What is the total value of the invoice?

2   A charity has hosted a fundraising event. It cost the charity £2,000 to host the event, and it sold tickets at £25.00 each.

   a   The charity sold 240 tickets. What is the value of the ticket sales?

   b   You have been asked to calculate the ratio of sales to expenses. The charity's total expenses from hosting the event were £2,000. What is the ratio of sales to expenses?

   c   Last year the charity hosted a similar event, but it only made $\frac{2}{3}$ of this year's sales. What was the value of the charity's sales last year?

3   A supermarket is reviewing its sales from the past five days. Its daily sales are below.

Monday	Tuesday	Wednesday	Thursday	Friday
£1,269.35	£1,500.95	£1,607.14	£1,659.16	£1,900.20

What is the average daily sales for the five-day period?

Practice assessment

Task 1.1

Organisations have assets, liabilities, income and expenditure.

a Which ONE of the following statements is true?

An asset is something an organisation owes. ☐

A liability is something an organisation owns. ☐

Income is something an organisation earns. ☑

b Place a tick (✓) in the appropriate column of the table below to show whether each of the items listed is an example of an asset, a liability, income or expenditure. You should not place more than one tick (✓) against each item.

Item	Asset	Liability	Income	Expenditure
Premises				
Motor vehicle tax				
Creditors				

Task 1.2

It is important to understand the terminology used when buying and selling goods for cash and on credit.

Choose the appropriate term from the list below to match the description.

Description	Term described
A transaction to sell services when payment is made immediately.	
A transaction to buy goods when the payment is made two weeks later.	

Terms: cash sale, cash purchase, credit sale, credit purchase, a debtor, a creditor

Task 1.3

Your organisation purchased 14 printer cartridges for £125.58 in total from JD Office Supplies.

a What is the cost of each printer cartridge?

£ ☐

JD Office Supplies agreed to issue an invoice asking your organisation to pay for the printer cartridges within 30 days.

b Is the purchase of the printer cartridges a cash transaction or a credit transaction?

☐

Task 1.4

Organisations issue and receive different documents when buying and selling goods.

Complete the following sentences by selecting the most appropriate option from the picklist below.

An organisation receives a [   ] from a supplier listing items returned to the supplier and showing the amount refunded.

When an organisation makes a payment to a supplier, the organisation sends a [   ] to the supplier detailing the items included in the payment.

An organisation receives a [   ] from a supplier for goods bought for cash.

Picklist: purchases credit note, purchases invoice, receipt, remittance advice

Task 1.5

You work for Reed Traders. You are preparing to record some documents in the books of prime entry.

a **Select which ONE of the documents below will be entered in the cash payments book.**

A cheque sent by a customer ☐

A credit note sent by a supplier ☐

A cheque sent to a supplier ☐

b **Select which ONE of the documents below will be entered in the sales returns daybook.**

A credit note sent to a customer ☐

A cheque sent by a customer ☐

An invoice sent to a customer ☐

PCS Ltd

6 Fox Way, Hatney, HN1 2GU

VAT Registration No. 247 8621 00

Invoice No. 1276

To: Reed Traders 14 July 20XX
41 Higher Street
Hatney, HN6 1TZ

	£
60 items of product LG @ £5 each	300.00
VAT @ 20%	60.00
Total	360.00

Terms: 30 days net   **Book of prime entry** [   ]

Marchant Ltd

22 The Street, Hatney, HN4 7UR

VAT Registration No. 456 1234 00   Credit note No. 56

To: Reed Traders 20 July 20XX
41 Higher Street
Hatney
HN6 1TZ

	£
8 items of product AB @ £4.50 each	36.00
VAT @ 20%	7.20
Total	43.20

Book of prime entry [   ]

Reed Traders

Cheques from customers listing

27 July 20XX

	£
J Dodd and Co	40.00
AB Ltd	129.50
Total	169.50

Book of prime entry [   ]

---

c Fill in the boxes on each document above to show which book of prime entry that document will be entered into. Select your answer from one of the following options.

Options: Cash payments book, Cash receipts book, Purchases daybook, Purchases returns daybook, Sales daybook, Sales returns daybook

Task 1.6

Some organisations use coding within the accounting records.

Show whether the following statement is true or false.

In a numerical coding system all codes consist of numbers only.

True ☐

False ☐

Task 1.7

Your organisation uses a batch processing system to enter sales invoices into the accounting records.

Show whether the following statement is true or false.

In a batch processing system sales invoices are grouped together and entered into the accounting records at the same time.

True ☐

False ☐

Task 1.8

On 18 July 20XX you have been asked to pay the following items into FPC Ltd's bank account.

Three £20 notes
Five £10 notes
Eight £2 coins
Nine 20 p coins

One cheque for £270.40

a **Complete the paying-in slip below.**

Date:	City Bank plc Redport	£50 notes	
		£20 notes	
		£10 notes	
	Account FPC Ltd	£5 notes	
		£2 coin	
		£1 coin	
	Paid in by AAT student	Other coin	
		Total cash	
		Cheques, POs	
	30-45-22 11240762	Total £	

b **Show whether the following statement is true or false.**

Paying-in slips should not be signed by the person who pays the items into the bank.

True ☐

False ☐

Task 1.9

It is important to ensure cheques sent to suppliers are completed properly.

On 12 July 20XX you are preparing a cheque for two hundred and twenty pounds and thirty pence to send to a supplier, Palmer Paints.

a **Which ONE of the following options shows the date as it should be written on the cheque?**

12 July ☐

21 July 20XX ☐

12 July 20XX ☐

b **Which ONE of the following options shows the payee as it should be written on the cheque?**

Pallmer ☐

Paints ☐

Palmer Paints ☐

c **Which ONE of the following options shows the amount in figures as it should be written on the cheque?**

222.30 ☐

202.33 ☐

220.30 ☐

d **Show whether the following statement is true or false.**

The amount written in figures on a cheque should be the same as the amount written in words.

True ☐

False ☐

Task 1.10

At the end of every year your organisation calculates the profit or loss for the year.

a **Show whether the following statement is true or false.**

Income plus expenditure equals profit.

True ☐

False ☐

Last year your organisation recorded income and expenditure as shown in the table below.

Income and expenditure	£
Sales	440,000
Cost of sales	286,500
Wages	26,080
Heat and light	8,760
Administration expenses	39,460

b **Use the income and expenditure figures to complete the following calculations.**

   i Calculate gross profit.

     £ ☐

   ii Calculate net profit.

     £ ☐

c **Using your answer from (b)(ii), calculate net profit as a percentage of sales. If your answer is not a whole number make sure you give your answer to two decimal places.**

   ☐ %

Task 1.11

An organisation is reviewing the selling price of some of its products.

The current selling price of product number 497 is £21.60. This is to be increased by $\frac{1}{6}$ (one sixth).

a **Calculate the increase in selling price for product number 497.**

   £ ☐

The current selling price of product number 214 is £11.40. This is to be increased by 5%.

b **Calculate the increase in selling price for product number 214.**

   £ ☐

Task 1.12

Your organisation keeps detailed records of costs.

Service and repair costs for each of four delivery vehicles are shown in the table below.

a **Complete the table to show the service and repair costs for Vehicle 3.**

Delivery vehicles	£
Vehicle 1	967.40
Vehicle 2	1,021.60
Vehicle 3	☐
Vehicle 4	848.00
Total	4,184.80

b **Calculate the average service and repair cost per vehicle.**

   £ ☐

Costs relating to the staff canteen are shown in the table below.

c **Complete the table to show the total canteen costs.**

Item	Cost £
Heat and light	194.60
Food and drink	1,624.00
Wages	476.50
Sundries	232.00
Total	

d **Calculate the ratio of the cost of food and drink to the cost of sundries.**

Select your answer from the following options.

Options: 8:1, 7:1, 6:1

Task 2.1

There are different types of business organisation.

Complete the following sentences by selecting the most appropriate option from the picklist below each sentence.

A large furniture retailer is a [   ] organisation.

Picklist: charitable, private sector, public sector

The primary purpose of the fire brigade is to [   ]

Picklist: make a loss, make a profit, provide a service

Task 2.2

It is important to understand the role of the accounts department within an organisation.

Show whether the following statements are true or false.

One role of an organisation's accounts department is to record the expenses of other departments within the organisation.

True ☐

False ☐

The customers of an organisation's accounts department are all from within the organisation.

True ☐

False ☐

Task 2.3

You work for AB Wholesalers. You have been asked to send an email to Dean James, the Sales Manager, advising him that sales last month were £30,000. You should also point out that this was £4,000 less than expected.

Use FIVE of the items below to produce an appropriate email.

From:	AATstudent@ABwholesalers.co.uk
To:	
Subject:	

Last munth sales were £4,000 less than you wanted. They were £30,000.	Regards AAT Student

Hello Dean	Sales figures	salesmanager@wholesalers.co.uk

Bye AAT student	Please be advised that last month total sales were £30,000. This was £4,000 less than expected.

deanjames@ABwholesalers.co.uk	Hi James	Last munth

Task 2.4

Organisations communicate using different styles and formats.

a Show whether the following statements are true or false.

It is not possible to use a template for letters sent to customers.

True ☐
False ☐

An internal set of guidelines for presenting documents is known as a house style.

True ☐
False ☐

You have been asked to inform all staff that the photocopier in reception is not working.

b **Select the most appropriate form of communication from the picklist.**

[   ]

Picklist: email, letter, report

Task 2.5

It is important to observe confidentiality.

Complete the following sentences by selecting the most appropriate option from the picklist below each sentence.

Confidential paperwork that is no longer needed should be

.

Picklist: put in the general waste, shredded, stored in an area accessible to all staff

The sickness records of individual members of staff should be accessible to

.

Picklist: all staff, accounts department staff only, authorised staff only

Task 2.6

Finance professionals and organisations have a duty to behave in a professional and socially responsible manner.

Choose the appropriate option to complete each sentence in the table below. You will not need to use all the options.

Sentence	Option
A qualified finance professional	
A finance professional must always	
A socially responsible organisation should provide	
An example of a socially responsible policy is to recommend	

Options

recycling facilities for waste paper

present information honestly

must continue to update technical knowledge

encourage employees to work after office hours and at weekends

need not undertake any more training

that the windows are shut when the heating system is in use

Task 2.7

Health and safety is important in the workplace.

a **Complete the following sentences by selecting the most appropriate option from the picklists below each sentence.**

have a responsiblity to work safely.

Picklist: Office staff, Managers, All staff

All hazards in the workplace should be reported
.

Picklist: at the end of the week, immediately, when someone is hurt

b   Show whether the following statements are true or false.

It is good practice to keep a tidy desk.

True ☐

False ☐

An organisation is not legally obliged to observe health and safety guidelines.

True ☐

False ☐

Task 2.8

It is important to understand the skills and attributes needed by a finance professional.

a   Complete the following sentence by selecting the most appropriate options from the picklist below each sentence.

A finance professional [   ] to communicate well.

Picklist: must always be able, does not have, may sometimes have

A finance professional [   ] good organisational skills.

Picklist: does not need, should have, may sometimes need

b   Show whether the following statements are true or false.

It is not beneficial for a trainee finance professional to discuss their training needs with a manager.

True ☐

False ☐

Job rotation is one way of acquiring new skills.

True ☐

False ☐

Task 2.9

It is important to work effectively.

Your colleague has just been asked to prepare a report by 5pm today. She asks you to help her as there is a lot of work to do.

a   Which ONE of the following actions should you take?

Refuse and tell your colleague it is not your responsiblity to help her. ☐

Check you have no outstanding tasks that must be completed today and agree to help. ☐

Agree to help but tell your colleague she must do some of your routine work tomorrow. ☐

Planning is very important to help you meet your deadlines.

b Show whether the following statement is true or false.

A work diary is not a planning aid.

True ☐

False ☐

It is important to use an appropriate form of communication at all times.

c Link each description to the appropriate form of communication by drawing a line from the left-hand box to the right-hand box. You should use each form of communication once only.

A communication sent to a new customer detailing your organisation's terms of business		Email
A non-urgent communication sent to all staff listing holiday dates for next year		Letter
An urgent communication sent to all staff telling them the lift is out of use		Memo

Task 2.10

- You work for Powell Printing.
- Today's date is 17 July 20XX.
- You have been asked to write a letter to a customer, Helen Peters, at JH Traders, Green Street, Barwood, BW6 7FD.
- You are to include a credit note for £1,200 to cancel invoice number 240.
- The invoice was in respect of the supply of advertising leaflets, which were returned on 16 July 20XX by the customer as the quality was poor.
- JH Traders is a good customer and you would like to continue to do business with them.

Use NINE of the options opposite to produce an appropriate letter.

17 July 20XX	Dear JH Traders	Return of poor quality advertising leaflets

Returned goods	Yours faithfully	The leafluts have been returned

Helen Peters
JH Traders
Green Street
Barwood
BW6 7FD

We enclose a credit note for £1,200 to cancel invoice number 240, which was issued in respect of the supply of these leaflets

Dear Helen

Please accept our apologies for the supply of poor quality advertising leaflets and thank you for returning them to us

16 July 20XX

We now enclose a credit note to cancel the invoice for the leaflets

Yours sincerely

We hope to continue to do business with you and assure you future products will be of a satisfactory quality

Mr Peters
JH Traders

We still want to do business with you

AAT Student
Accounts Assistant

Powell Printing
4 Hart Street
Shockley
SK6 1TZ

Glossary

Abbreviated language Shorthands commonly used in texting, such as "tnt" instead of "tonight".

Accounting professionals People who have qualifications in accountancy. They are usually members of a professional body such as the AAT.

Accurate The ability to complete and review work without making mistakes.

Alphabetical codes Codes that only use letters.

Alphanumerical codes Codes that use letters and numbers.

Appropriate Correct for the purpose it is required for.

Assets Items of value owned by an organisation.

Authority Having permission from the person who "owns" the information to hold or use this data.

Average An average is the number that best represents the typical value of a series of numbers. It is sometimes called the "mean".

Bank loan A fixed amount of money an organisation borrows from a bank.

Batch processing Entering batches of financial documents all together rather than individually.

Behaviour How a person conducts themself.

Cash paid listing A list of all cash paid by an organisation, detailing the date, name of payee and the amount paid.

Cash payments book A record of all an organisation's expenditure.

Cash purchase An organisation pays the supplier for items of expenditure at the time of purchase.

Cash receipts book A record of all income received by an organisation.

Cash received listing A list of all cash received by an organisation, detailing the date, the name of the business or person making the payment and the amount received.

Cash sale The customer pays for goods or services at the time of the sale.

Cash transactions Goods or services are paid for at the time of purchase.

Charities Organisations set up to raise money and awareness to promote a particular cause and to provide services for specific groups.

Cheque A method of payment in which a person (or organisation) instructs a bank to transfer a specified sum of money from their bank account to the bank account of the recipient of the cheque. This instruction is made by writing a cheque.

Cheques paid listing A list of all cheques paid by an organisation, detailing the date, name of payee and the amount paid.

Cheques received listing A list of all cheques received by an organisation, detailing the date, the name of the business or person making the payment and the amount received.

Closing salutation The end of a letter or an email. In letters this will either be "Yours sincerely" or "Yours faithfully". In emails it is more common to use "Regards".

Communicate The process of transmitting information from one person to another.

Communication The process of transferring information between two or more people. They may communicate information in verbal, written or diagrammatic form.

Confidential Private or sensitive. The term is often applied to financial and personal information that must be kept secret or only made available to certain people.

Consistent To keep something the same. For example, most organisations insist that their letters have a consistent look, by setting rules about where the organisation's logo appears, the font that can be used, and so on.

Contingency An alternative plan in case something changes. In a schedule, it is common to keep some contingency time in case one stage runs late.

Cost of sales The direct cost of producing the goods and services that have been sold. For example, raw materials for a manufacturing organisation, or products to sell for a retailing organisation. Organisations that provide services often have a very small cost of sales.

Credit note A note informing the customer of any amounts refunded by the supplier following the return of goods or errors on a previous invoice. The credit note can be used against outstanding invoices.

Creditor A person or business to whom an organisation owes money. A creditor is a liability because the money belongs to another person or business.

Credit purchase An organisation pays the supplier for items of expenditure some time after making the purchase. The supplier is now a creditor of the organisation.

Credit sale The customer is allowed to pay for the goods or services some time after the sale. The customer is now a debtor of the organisation.

Credit transactions Payment for goods or services is delayed until some time after the purchase.

Debtor A person or business that owes money to an organisation. A debtor is an asset because the money belongs to the organisation even though it has not actually received it yet.

Decimals A fraction of a number that is written using the decimal system. This is indicated by the use of the decimal point (.).

Denominator The number on the bottom of the fraction.

Disclosing Letting others see or access private information.

Document An electronic or written piece of information, such as an email, letter or report.

Effective working practices Ways of working that help people complete tasks accurately and on time.

Efficiently Completing work as quickly as possible to the required standards without making mistakes.

Environmental Relating to the natural world and our physical surroundings.

Ethical The correct and acceptable way of doing something.

Expenditure The amount of money paid by an organisation to purchase goods and services.

External customer A person from outside the organisation who requests information from the accounts department.

Formal Following accepted rules and conventions. Formal language and communication follows the rules of grammar and spelling.

Fraction A way of showing a part of a whole number without presenting it as a decimal.

Function An activity carried out in an organisation, often in a department of the same name. For example, the sales function is usually carried out by sales teams in the sales department.

Gross profit The profit (or amount of money left) from sales after the cost of sales has been deducted.

Health and safety The process of reducing risk in the workplace through safe practices, training and written rules.

House style A set of guidelines that state how to organise and present documents.

Income The amount of money received by an organisation from its sales.

Induction A training period when an employee starts to work for a new employer.

Informal Less structured and conventional. Informal language and communication is less structured than formal communications.

Integrity Demonstrating honesty and adopting an approach to work guided by strong moral principles.

Internal customer A person from inside the organisation who requests financial information from the organisation's accounts department.

Invoice A document sent by the supplier to the customer listing the goods supplied and requesting payment for these goods.

Legal In keeping with the law.

Liable Responsible under law.

Liability Money owed by an organisation to other organisations, businesses and individuals.

Literate Being skilled at dealing with written content.

Loss When an organisation spends more money than it earns.

Monies A collective term used to describe different forms of payments and receipts including cash, cheques and direct bank transfers.

Net profit The amount left from sales income (gross profit) after cost of sales and all other expenses (such as wages, electricity and marketing costs) have been deducted.

Numerate Being skilled at dealing with numbers.

Numerator The number on the top of the fraction.

Numerical codes Codes that only use numbers.

Opening salutation A greeting in a letter or an email, usually starting "Dear" in a letter and "Hello" in an email.

Overdraft An arrangement that allows an organisation to take more money out of its bank account than it has on deposit.

Payee The person the cheque is written to.

Paying-in slip A form used to pay cash and cheques into a bank account.

Peer Someone with a similar level of authority to you within the organisation.

Policy A written document explaining how an organisation does something and the procedures it follows.

Private sector The part of the economy consisting of privately owned businesses that are set up to make a profit. These include sole traders, partnerships and limited companies.

Profit The amount of money an organisation earns after all expenses have been deducted from turnover.

Professional A person who is qualified to carry out a task with a high level of expertise and skill.

Professional journals Typically magazine-style publications written specifically for professionals in accounting positions. Journals contain information on significant changes in the accounting world, along with practical advice on how to complete particular tasks efficiently.

Professionalism Demonstrating a high level of competence in your work and meeting the required standards of the profession.

Professionally Completed or undertaken to acceptable standards, agreed conventions and with no mistakes.

Public sector The part of the economy consisting of publicly owned organisations that provide services to citizens. These organisations are paid for through taxation.

Purchase order A document sent to a supplier detailing the goods that the customer wants to purchase.

Purchases daybook A record of all invoices received from suppliers.

Purchases returns daybook A record of all credit notes received from suppliers.

Ratio The amount of one number in relation to another number. The numbers are always separated by a colon (:).

Receipt A document given as proof of a cash transaction.

Remittance advice A document sent to inform the supplier that an invoice has been paid.

Responsible A duty of care over something or someone.

Routine Something you will do every day

Sales daybook A record of all invoices sent out to customers.

Sales income The money coming into an organisation from sales of goods and services. For a single product, income can be calculated by multiplying the number of items sold by the price of the item.

Sales returns daybook A record of all credit notes sent out to customers.

Securing Protecting information against unauthorised access.

Shareholders The owners of limited companies. They invest money in a company in the hope that it will make a profit, so they will get a return on the money they invested.

Signatory/Signatories A person or persons who are authorised to sign cheques on behalf of an organisation.

Slang Informal language that is more commonly used in spoken communication than written documents.

SMART target A target that is specific, measurable, achievable, realistic and timed.

Standards A minimum expected level of quality that your work must reach.

Statement of account A document that summarises the transactions between a supplier and customer. It shows the invoices and credit notes sent, payments received and any outstanding balance on the account.

Support To provide help and information to another function within the organisation.

Sustainability The process of acting in a way that won't compromise the future. This means ensuring that what we do today doesn't prevent people from doing something in the future.

Template A pre-prepared document on a computer drive that allows users to create business communications with a consistent presentation.

Time management The process of organising your time so that tasks are completed by a given deadline

Work plan A list of jobs to complete, organised into the order in which they will be tackled and the time when each will be completed.

Work shadowing The process of following a more experienced member of staff around so that the junior member of staff picks up skills and ideas on how to do their own job more successfully.